Praise for *Loving Conflict*

"*Loving Conflict* conveys Anna's conviction that conflict, much like tango, approached with hope and compassion sparks stronger, more empathetic leadership."

—JESUS DE LA GARZA, founder and creator, Monarch Leaders; Nuevo León, Mexico

"Building stakeholder-centered organizations requires something most leaders haven't been taught: the ability to hold space for competing interests without collapsing into compromise. Anna Lecat's five principles give leaders practical tools to navigate these tensions with presence and purpose. *Loving Conflict* is the missing manual for anyone trying to create collaboration across diverse stakeholder ecosystems."

—KENT GREGOIRE, executive consultant specializing in regenerative business operating systems; Massachusetts, United States

"Anya offers a wise, generous guide to seeing conflict not as a problem to fix but as an unexpected doorway into deeper connection. This book shows the reader how to recognize difficulties and tension as portals to deeper connection and growth, revealing what we've been longing to understand about ourselves and each other."

—CECILY MAK, author, *Undimmed: The Eight Awarenesses for Freedom from Unwanted Habits*; California, United States

"Through *Loving Conflict,* Anna has helped me understand that conflict, internal and external, is the birthplace of change and connection. Her work has empowered me to lean in and embrace it fully."

—RENEE RUSSO, "The Exit Queen;" CEO, Rise Up Business Coaching; Vancouver, Canada

"*Loving Conflict* teaches us how to resolve conflict with grace and dignity while building trust in the process. It is a must-have playbook for navigating life's trickiest moments."

—JOSH GARDNER, CEO and cofounder,
Kung Fu Data; Singapore, Singapore

"Anna has an extraordinary way of turning conflict into something meaningful, even hopeful. Her stories stay with you, her practices strengthen you, and her perspective softens the edges we all carry. She reveals how tension can become a doorway rather than a dead end and how curiosity can transform even the most difficult conversations. Her perspective is generous, grounding, and beautifully human."

—SYLVIE DI GIUSTO, CSP, CPAE, international
3D immersive Hall of Fame keynote
speaker; Florida, United States

"Anna's work did not just teach me how to navigate conflict; it changed the way I live. Her methods helped me walk into hard conversations with clarity, courage, and a wide open heart. I have used her tools in my marriage, my friendships, my leadership, and in the moments where everything felt on the line. *Loving Conflict* is the guide for anyone who is ready to stop avoiding tension and start transforming through it."

—JENNY FETEROVICH, executive producer,
START UP TV show, Parliament Studios; global
learning community host, Entrepreneur's
Organization; Michigan, United States

"*Loving Conflict* gave me something I have never had before. It showed me a simple and compassionate way to move toward conflict with more confidence instead of fear. Anna's stories and tools changed how I show up in moments I used to avoid."

—IVY GUSTAFSON, thought leader advisor and
speaker coach; founder, Ivy Gustafson
Advisory; Florida, United States

"Anna's book is so precious to me because it offers concrete paths to the craft of peace, which can transform our lives and change the world. Yes, even from conflict, astonishing fruitfulness can emerge! But we must take the necessary steps. Thank you, Anna, for sharing your experience with us and opening paths of hope. A must-read and a must-live!"

—FR. ANTOINE-EMMANUEL, Catholic monk;
Basilique de Vézelay, France

"What if we knew how to resolve disagreements without blaming or shaming? What if we had the grace and confidence to dance with conflict? If any of that sounds good, you're in the right place as that is what this inspiring book teaches. Read it and reap."

—SAM HORN, founder and CEO, The Intrigue
Agency; author of ten books; Texas, United States

"One of my most trusted spiritual guides said to me years ago, 'go toward what you are resisting.' Every time I read/hear Anna Lecat's words, every moment that I'm in her luminous orbit, I'm reminded of the deeply challenging and sacred nature of facing our fears, of stepping into zones of discomfort and looking conflict straight in the eye. Because of Anna's old-growth wisdom and guidance, hope is seeded, healing manifests, and life is reaffirmed. The redemptive stories and lessons packed into this book tether you to life and remind you what really matters."

—RABBI MICHAEL LEZAK, Center for
Social Justice, GLIDE; California, United States

"This book is sorely needed by our planet on a societal level and a personal level. Imagine a world where each of us didn't avoid messy conflicts but approached them with love and curiosity. The goal isn't to be right; it's to bring about transformation internally and externally. Do yourself a favor and get this book."

—DR. KINARI WEBB, author, *Guardians of the
Trees: A Journey of Hope Through Healing
the Planet*; co-author, *The Art of Radical Listening:
Revealing Collective Wisdom for Change*,
California, United States

"In *Loving Conflict*, Anna Lecat reveals that conflict is not a battle to win but a tango to enter—where presence, rhythm, and shared humanity transform tension into connection. Her wisdom invites us to move through our hardest moments with more courage, compassion, and artistry. This book is a gift for every leader, parent, partner, and human who wants to build a more compassionate world."

—**MELISSA DAVIS,** leadership advisor; Enneagram expert; founder, Melissa Davis Co; Florida, United States

"Anna Lecat has an extraordinary gift for turning conflict into connection. Drawing from a life lived across cultures, she invites us to lower our walls, listen more deeply, and see the humanity in one another. *Loving Conflict* is the hopeful, practical guide leaders, partners, and communities need right now."

—**STEPHANIE CAMARILLO,** global speaker, transformation guide, and entrepreneur; Idaho, United States

"*Loving Conflict* is a remarkable guide for anyone who has spent a lifetime avoiding difficult conversations. Anna reveals the deeper patterns behind our fear of conflict and shows us how presence, curiosity, and the courage to speak our truth can turn tension into genuine collaboration. This book teaches us that when we don't honor who we are, we lose ourselves in the conformity of others—yet when we dare to engage, we reclaim connection, clarity, and freedom."

—**TANYA CHERNOVA,** award-winning speaker, best-selling author; Toronto, Canada

"A powerful and necessary book. Anna's message on *Loving Conflict*—first shared at TEDxGraz—offers leaders the human-centered future skills our world urgently needs: creating safety, embracing tension, and turning differences into insight. Her clarity and warmth make this work indispensable for anyone striving to build a better way of living and working together."

—**KAROLA SAKOTNIK,** architect of positive future; keynote speaker; founder, Future Skills Farming; best-selling author; Styria, Austria

"*Loving Conflict* reframes one of the hardest parts of leadership into one of its most valuable. Anna Lecat shows that conflict isn't a failure of alignment; it's often the doorway to real collaboration. Grounded in lived experience, this book offers practical principles you can use across leadership, partnerships, and teams. It's not about winning arguments; it's about presence, better questions, and building trust when it matters most. For founders and operators navigating high-stakes decisions, *Loving Conflict* is a clear, humane guide to doing the real work of working with people."

—JOANNA LING, Group CEO, PE Holdings; Sarawak, Malaysia

"Anna Lecat offers a radical yet practical call to lovingly embrace conflict in our relationships as the optimal means of reaching true collaboration. She provides clear, concise, and simple instruction for each of us to achieve the collaborative outcomes we desire."

—MEG CARLSON, entrepreneur, former
Fortune 100 executive; Idaho, United States

"As an organization committed to the practice of courageous citizenship, we know at Braver Angels that true collaboration is not the absence of conflict; it is the willingness to engage it with courage and skill. Anna Lecat's *Loving Conflict* is the essential blueprint for this transformation. Lecat challenges us to step into the divide. This book provides the framework for that courageous work. Her Five Principles of Loving Conflict are the foundational skills we must cultivate to move past fear and defense. The concept of Extreme Listening is a powerful mirror for our own invitation at Braver Angels to see the person behind the political label. Crucially, Lecat addresses the fact that the conflicts we avoid creating are often the ones that need us most, urging us to be the one 'brave enough to start' the difficult conversation. This is the definitive, action-oriented practice guide you need. Highly recommended."

—MAURY GILES, CEO, Braver Angels; Utah, United States

"We all have something that rots inside: unspoken disagreements. Hurt and anger gnaw at our relations because we fear conflict. Families breed hatred, businesses succumb to endless frustrations, countries prepare for war. Conflict is bad, we are told. Yes, it is, says Anna, when we ignore it. Anna's book flips the conflict issue on its head. Just go for it. Love it. Read!"

—NATACHA KUCIC, film producer and storyteller; founder and CEO, First Draft; Madrid, Spain

"A rare book on how to dance with conflict and learn to turn tension into curiosity, flow, and relationships that grow stronger through difference."

—ANDREAS KONSTANTINOU, CEO, SlashData; Attiki, Greece

"Anna Lecat has been a game-changing advisor to me on the most challenging communication issues within my organization as well as in personal matters. I'm grateful for this gem of a book, which I will now gift to everyone I know. "

—MARINA BYEZHANOVA, CEO, Brand of a Leader; Montréal-Ouest, Canada

"Throughout my life I've thought that my ability to avoid conflict was an asset, but in reality, it has been holding me back, both at work and in my personal relationships. Anna Lecat's *Loving Conflict* is a must-read for anyone who shies away from conflict and who seeks a more authentic, and ultimately more productive, approach to the dance of life."

—MARYAM MOHIT, author, former tech exec, TBI advocate; California, USA

LOVING CONFLICT

Creating Collaboration Where Others See Division

ANNA LECAT

River Grove
BOOKS

Published by River Grove Books
Austin, TX
www.rivergrovebooks.com

Distributed by River Grove Books

Design and composition by Greenleaf Book Group and Teresa Muniz
Cover design by Greenleaf Book Group and Teresa Muniz
Cover images used under license from ©AdobeStock/Vikivector

Publisher's Cataloging-in-Publication data is available.

Print ISBN: 978-1-966629-97-9

eBook ISBN: 978-1-966629-98-6

First Edition

*To my family, given and chosen, my parents,
my husband, our three children, and Hong Zhou.*

*Our hardest conversations teach me to stay close,
love deeply, and fight kindly.*

CONTENTS

Introduction

SURROUNDED BY CONFLICT

Anya was born to a Jewish family living in what was then Soviet Ukraine. It was the late seventies, and life had brought many challenges for her parents. Russian culture had been imposed, and members of ethnic minorities like Anya's parents often faced pressures to conform. Resources were scarce and anti-Semitism was quietly present in both state policies and in society itself.

As Ukrainian Jews, Anya's parents experienced a unique mix of cultural assimilation and discrimination. Russian culture and language were deeply entrenched in schools, workplaces, and public life, making it difficult for them to openly express their Ukrainian identity or Jewish traditions. While speaking Ukrainian or practicing Jewish customs wasn't outright forbidden, it was certainly not encouraged, as the Soviet state prioritized a Russian-centric identity. Anti-Semitism added another layer to their lives. Jewish people often encountered barriers in housing, education, and employment.

Anya grew up knowing what it meant to wait. She remembers standing with her mother in endless lines, holding her hand tight while they waited for milk, for bread, for whatever was available that day. Even as a small child, she understood there were things you said out loud and things you kept to yourself. The world beyond their borders felt like something from a fairy tale, unreachable and mysterious.

While this environment made it challenging to fully embrace their Ukrainian-Jewish heritage, her parents found ways to preserve their identity in the privacy of their home. They passed down their culture, history, and traditions, quietly maintaining their heritage despite the subtle pressures around them. They found quiet ways to keep their sanity and joy alive and vibrant.

Anya became part of a rich communal and cultural life due to the conscious efforts of her parents. They, with their large group of friends, artists, musicians, writers, and university professors, organized parties every weekend. Anya grew up hearing the sounds of a guitar, people singing and harmonizing, grown-ups reading poetry in the midst of laughter and friendly joking, and dancing would last all night long.

Anya was told she was beautiful. Her mom, Svetlana, somehow intuitively understood the importance of self-love and self-confidence, and fed it to Anya in generous portions daily.

Anya's father, Kim, sprinkled humor everywhere he went as a way of coping with the very unsettled and difficult life he was dealt. He would often teach his children, "Question everything and everyone. Don't follow the status quo. Especially don't follow the crowd."

This type of thinking was actually dangerous at the time. It was not wise to stand out, to question the government. Yet Anya's parents did. They read forbidden books, listened to music that was not approved by the authorities, discussed the history of religions and philosophies, and even became entrepreneurs before it was allowed for people to do so.

So, in spite of her surroundings, Anya grew up with an understanding of open-mindedness, ideas about freedom of expression, and the notion of *radical questioning* as her normal.

But when she was sent to kindergarten at the age of four, imagine her disbelief when every morning started the same way. The school director had all the kids line up. She then said, "Children, let's all answer this very important question in one voice: Who is the biggest, most horrible villain in the world?"

And all fifty kids would chant loudly: "Ro-nald Rea-gan! Ro-nald Rea-gan!"

Anya was mortified. First of all, she knew there was no way she was joining in. At just four years old, she was not sure why, yet she knew that what they were doing was wrong. And she had lots of questions: "Who is Ronald Reagan? Why is he the most horrible villain in the world? Where does he live? Can I go meet him?" No one at the kindergarten wanted to answer her questions. She felt alone with her queries and sensed she didn't quite belong with the rest of the kids who were happy to join in with the chanting.

Yet, her natural curiosity, friendliness, and warm heart tugged at her to connect with the others in spite of how she felt. To connect with the people who saw her as someone other and different from them. Even at that early age, thanks to the love she received at home, it was intuitive for her to think, "I can learn a great deal from people who are different from me. And I can influence people's judgments by showing them who I am."

So when six-year-old Anya woke up excited for her first day of primary school, she carried all of this with her: the music from those weekend gatherings, the laughter, the absolute certainty that she was loved exactly as she was. She had no idea her parents were about to ask her to hide the thing that made her most proud. It came as a surprise, then, when they sat her down right before leaving their home that day and said: "Anya, please, no matter what happens at school, do not tell anyone we are Jewish. It will be dangerous for us if people know that."

Anya was confused, disappointed, and angry. "Why do I have to hide who I am? And are you telling me to actually lie?"

When it was her turn to get up in front of the full class and her teacher to introduce herself, Anya was petrified, shaking, and yet determined. She did what her father taught her so well. She questioned what he had told her to do.

She stood up and said, "Hello! My name is Anya, and I am Jewish!" Everyone heard her shaky yet passionate voice, and they saw her face turning bright red as she saw the shocked expressions on the faces of the teacher and her classmates. No one had ever spoken with such uncontested, shameless pride.

But her bravery had consequences, putting her front and center in the conflicts that were embedded in the culture at the time. Being the only openly Jewish child in that school meant becoming a target. The teasing came in all forms. Sometimes whispers, sometimes shouts. Jokes that weren't really jokes. The kind of cruelty that children learn from the adults around them without even knowing it. Even when people said things that were supposed to be "harmless," Anya was still hurt by the comments. There were many moments of exclusion, like being left out of games during recess or not being included in group activities or social gatherings. She was often perceived as different, and her best friend would often say to her, "I hate all the Jews, but you are okay."

Over time, Anya became "my Jewish friend" for many. She invited her friends to her house and exposed them to her family culture. Her friends got to explore the huge library that her parents had assembled over the years. They stayed for hours listening to her father tell them stories about the world or Greek myths or the history of arts, or they'd simply discuss the books they were reading and he'd offer his wise and often witty perspective. They were invited to the lively family gatherings.

Anya's parents treated everyone equally and always had their house and their dining table open to visitors, so there were always interesting people around ready to talk to the children or help them with their homework or even matters of the heart that might be bothering them. Anya's friends also got to witness the strong, nurturing bonds that existed between the generations of her family, with both her parents being close to their parents, and with the grandparents being an active part of the family life. Step by step, her friends went from "I hate all the Jews, but you are okay" to "We just love spending time with you and your family, we learn so much here" and ultimately to "I am sorry for what I said about you in the past. I love and respect you."

I am Anya. That little girl was me.

I often reflect on how those early days as part of a persecuted minority shaped my life. I could have, like every other Jewish child in my elementary school, listened to my parents and stayed below the radar. And what if I had done that? What if I had not chosen to step into the conflict, to try to connect with children who were raised so differently from me? I can barely imagine how much poorer my life would have been. Throughout my life, I've seen how every divide can be reframed as an invitation to learn something essential. Personal divides, professional ones, cultural differences. All of them. And that's why I've learned to love conflict. Not violence. Not war. Not aggression. Rather the conflict in hard conversations. The tension. The moments most people run away from. Because conflict is where real collaboration begins.

WHAT DOES IT MEAN TO LOVE CONFLICT?

People often ask me, "Anna, why 'love' conflict? Why not just 'engage' it or 'handle' it?" The word *love* feels too strong, too risky, too much.

When I'm just *engaging* conflict, it feels like work. I do it because I have to, because avoiding it is worse. I grit my teeth, have the difficult conversation, and hope it ends quickly.

When I'm *loving* conflict, it feels like coming alive. I do it because it's where real understanding happens, where I discover what people actually care about beneath their positions.

I've learned to recognize the physical difference. When I'm just engaging in conflict, my body gets tight and protective. When I'm loving conflict, my body gets energized and open. My heart rate goes up not from fear but from anticipation. What am I about to learn? What blind spot is about to be revealed?

Loving conflict means getting excited when someone sees things differently because you're about to learn something. It means feeling energized by tension instead of drained by it.

But loving conflict does *not* mean seeking out arguments for the sake of arguing, enjoying hurting people, creating drama where none exists, or abandoning your own needs to keep others comfortable.

The goal of this book isn't to teach you to tolerate conflict or manage it skillfully. It's to help you fall in love with the process of working through differences with people who matter to you.

Every relationship that has ever meant anything to me has been deepened through conflict, not despite it.

> *Every relationship that has ever meant anything to me has been deepened through conflict, not despite it.*

Reassurance: What Loving Conflict Does NOT Mean

If you're reading this book with some apprehension, wondering if I'm asking you to become more argumentative or confrontational, let me put your mind at ease. Learning to love conflict is not about

- Being aggressive or combative
- Starting fights or creating drama
- Always having to speak your mind
- Becoming someone you're not
- Losing your natural kindness or empathy
- Turning every disagreement into a debate

Loving conflict means developing the skills to engage differences productively when they arise naturally. It means not running away from tension that's already there. It means trusting that you can disagree with someone and still care about them deeply.

WHEN LOVING CONFLICT GOES SIDEWAYS

Here's what I wish someone had told me when I started this work. Not every attempt to love conflict goes beautifully. Some of my biggest failures have taught me as much as my successes.

A few years ago, I was working with a family business in France where the father and son had been stuck in conflict for months about their company's direction. I was convinced that if I could just get them to see each other's humanity, everything would work out.

I pushed too hard, too fast. I asked them to do vulnerable sharing exercises before they felt safe. I encouraged the son to express his frustration with his father's approach. I thought I was helping them break through. Instead, I was creating breakdown.

The father felt attacked and humiliated in front of his employees. The son felt exposed and unsupported when his father shut down completely. They left that session more divided than when they'd arrived. The father ended our contract the next day.

What I learned from that failure changed how I approach conflict. Loving conflict doesn't mean pushing people toward vulnerability they're not ready for. It doesn't mean exposing people's deepest fears in front of others. It doesn't mean assuming that more honesty is always better.

Sometimes loving conflict means going slower. Sometimes it means working with people separately before bringing them together. Sometimes it means respecting people's defenses instead of trying to break them down.

That French family did eventually work through their issues, though not with my help. The son later told me that our failed session had shown them they needed to approach their differences more carefully, with more respect for each other's dignity.

Even my failures taught them something about loving conflict. Sometimes the lesson is what not to do.

BRIDGING DIVIDES

Right now, our world can feel more divided than ever. We're bombarded by narratives driving us apart, ranging from the profound (political ideologies that seem entrenched, cultural differences depicted as insurmountable) to the mundane (did that driver really just cut you off in traffic?). But if you look closely, it's easy to find people who want to bridge those divides. They want to find ways to live in a civil society where people of different ideas can still work together and collaborate despite conflicts between them.

Are you one of those people? If so, I hope you will find both inspiration and practical guidance in this book. We'll explore stories of people who have stepped into conflict to create understanding and opportunities for collaboration.

You'll encounter Hope: eight people with eight perspectives, Palestinians, Jews, Muslims, and Christians, staying in conversation when it would be easier to walk away. You'll also witness profound breakthroughs both large and small, such as a KKK member surrendering his robe and a husband learning how to interact more effectively with his wife. These are not isolated miracles; they are blueprints for what's possible when we learn to love conflict for the opportunities it provides.

Loving conflict is not easy. It requires tools and practice, just like any other skill. In Part I of this book, I'll share stories that set the framework for what's possible when conflict is seen as an opportunity rather than a barrier. Part II describes five principles that create a framework of practical steps you can take and techniques for learning to love conflict. In Part III, I'll share some profound examples of what happens when people are willing to reach across the divides created by conflict.

Each chapter invites active engagement, guiding you step-by-step through practices designed to enrich your interactions and relationships. From prioritizing genuine, face-to-face social interactions to intentionally managing digital distractions, each tool is ready for immediate implementation into your daily routine.

I'll share practical reflections, like how consciously removing my phone from sight during face-to-face interactions has protected precious moments of human connection.

Loving conflict is not about changing minds but expanding hearts. It's less about winning arguments and more about truly seeing each other. It's about learning to use the energy surrounding conflict to grow deep roots of understanding.

Our world doesn't need more arguments. It needs more conversations.

It doesn't need more division. It needs more understanding.

It doesn't need more certainty. It needs more curiosity.

Those are the goals I hope you'll pursue with me in *Loving Conflict*. Learning to create genuine collaboration through the conflicts we used to avoid.

If You Already Want to Stop Reading

I get it. If the idea of loving conflict still feels impossible, that makes complete sense. You might be thinking, "Anna, this sounds exhausting. I barely have energy for the conflicts I can't avoid. Why would I want more of them?"

Most of us learned early that conflict equals danger. Our nervous systems are designed to avoid what feels threatening. I felt the same way.

You're not creating conflict by reading this book. Conflict is already happening in your life. The question is whether you're going to develop skills to engage it productively or continue to let it drain your energy through avoidance.

I used to think avoiding conflict would give me more peace. Instead, I spent years walking on eggshells, feeling disconnected from people I cared about. The conflicts didn't disappear. They just went underground and got messier.

Stay with me for the next few chapters. You don't have to love conflict by the end of this book. You just have to be willing to get curious about it.

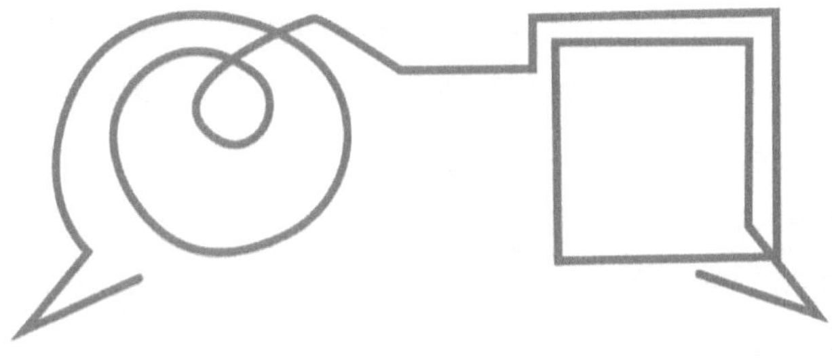

THE TANGO OF CONFLICT AND COLLABORATION

For many years, people have come to me with the same request: They want help dealing with others whose beliefs differ from their own. Spouses. Parents and children. Business partners. People from opposite political parties. They all want the same thing. To find a way to get along without so much conflict.

I used to think my job was helping them avoid conflict to create collaboration. I was wrong. Now I know the truth. It's *through the conflict* that we create genuine collaboration.

Our world loves emphasizing differences and turning disagreements into walls. But what if those walls are actually doorways? What if the very conflicts we're trying to avoid are exactly what we need to create the collaboration we're seeking?

I feel compelled at this point to reveal that I love to dance, especially tango. It's one of my main languages and modalities of self-expression and creativity. This is my way to process my feelings and emotions, digest hard events and reflect on difficult realities, and connect deeply with other people without words.

In tango, two people who might seem like opposing forces come together. They don't avoid the tension between them. They use it to create something beautiful. This is what collaboration through conflict looks like. Different styles, different energies, different ways of moving through the world. But when they connect, when they truly listen to each other through touch and movement, they create something bigger than either dancer could achieve alone. Art.

This is exactly how I see conflict and collaboration. Not as enemies, but as dance partners creating something beautiful together.

In this section of the book, I want to dispel the myth that conflict prevents collaboration. Using stories from my own experiences and those of others, I'll cover the following points:

- We can influence the balance between conflict and collaboration by making choices that influence how we deal with the tension between the two (Chapter 1: Elevating Out of Conflict).

- To be able to learn from conflict, we have to adopt "intellectual humility," the willingness to believe that our knowledge and understanding are not perfect and that we can learn from others (Chapter 2: Is It Possible My Understanding Is Flawed?).

Together, these two mindsets create a foundation for learning the practical techniques of loving conflict that I'll discuss later in the book.

Chapter 1

ELEVATING OUT OF CONFLICT

My husband Jerome and I were in Paris late one rainy, cold, and dark November evening at the busy and crowded La Défense gas station, waiting in a line to add air to our tires. We had our three small children in the car, who were hungry and tired, ready to get home and rest after their busy day at school. The line looked hopelessly long at the station, and everyone was irritated and on the edge.

So was this motorcycle driver who tried to cut us off to get air into his motorcycle tires first. He had his girlfriend on the back, and he was putting on the tough-guy show as he ignored everyone's disapproving stares.

I saw my Jerome's eyebrows raise in disbelief and his jaws tense up. He was ready to go to battle. And then I watched him do what he does so well. Jerome slowed down his breathing, waiting for his face and his body to relax. I watched him take a deep breath and smile. Then he lowered our windows and told the motorcycle driver in a soft friendly voice: "Please go ahead and get in line in front of us. You only have two tires to pump, and you guys are getting cold and wet. We are fine here inside the car; we can wait."

The looks on their faces were priceless. Disbelief, a bit of guilt, but mostly relief, joy, and wonder.

Jerome is a master of elevating himself and others and being deliberate about it. He's always cared about this particular skill and spent years with mentors and coaches practicing and refining it. Jerome managed to master his emotions, assess the situation, and question the usual response behavior that is normally the default. He did not respond to their behavior with what would have been a totally understandable and expected response, which would have further escalated the situation. Jerome stopped himself and was truly deliberate about his choice of action. The tension was relieved with kindness and grace. A stressful situation was resolved, and as a result, he taught a precious lesson to our kids. He gifted inspiration to me, and in turn, I am able to gift it to you.

Jerome showed me exactly what it means to elevate out of conflict. He made the conscious choice to rise above the immediate tension of a confrontation rather than being pulled deeper into it.

When we elevate, we shift from reactive emotions to thoughtful response. We create space between our feelings and our actions, allowing us to see the situation from a higher perspective. This doesn't mean avoiding the conflict or surrendering our position; it means approaching it from a place of clarity rather than chaos.

Elevation transforms conflict from a battlefield to a conversation. It's a skill that some people seem to practice naturally, while others of us need to develop it deliberately through practice and awareness. At its core, elevation is about loving conflict enough to stay present when we're triggered, because that's how we create collaboration where others see only division.

You'll see this kind of elevation in stories throughout this text. Here, I want to focus on understanding what's going on at the moment where we find ourselves giving conflict the leading role in the dance.

I learned what elevating out of conflict really looks like during a board meeting I was leading in San Francisco. Two cofounders were in a heated argument about the company's direction. Voices were raised, accusations were flying, and everyone else was sitting there uncomfortably.

Then one of them stopped mid-sentence and said, "Wait. We're both fighting for the same thing. We want this company to succeed. Can we start over?"

The room went quiet. Instead of continuing the battle, he had chosen to elevate. He acknowledged their shared goal instead of focusing on their disagreement about how to get there.

The tone in the room changed. Instead of a fight about who was right, it became a conversation about which path would actually work better. They still disagreed, but they were disagreeing as partners trying to solve the same problem, not as enemies trying to defeat each other.

This is what elevating out of conflict looks like. Not avoiding the disagreement but choosing to approach it from a higher perspective.

THE POWER OF SPLIT-SECOND DECISIONS

When we are in the midst of a conflict or a confrontation, and I'm specifically talking about when we are triggered by the other person, we make a split-second decision to either escalate or to de-escalate. We all recognize when this happens. It is often the moment when we suddenly feel a rush of heat to our face or our heart beating wildly or our hands shaking. Maybe our vision even becomes blurred. It gets so uncomfortable inside our body that all we want is for the intense discomfort to go away.

We can rush into the fight and attack the other person. This may feel most intuitive to us. Fight, attack, protect ourselves, stop the other party from saying what triggers us so much. The other way is to de-escalate. We need to elevate ourselves out of the conflict zone and into a conversation zone where we can actually hear the other person and talk calmly. We know deep down that de-escalation is what is needed. At some point, we hopefully have all experienced the great benefits of calm conversation where both parties listen and are listened to, and where solutions have a chance to be found.

And yet we find choosing de-escalation so hard. It's not the muscle many of us work very often. And that's why the stories of people actually flexing these muscles are so touching and resonant to us.

My dear friend Christina Harbridge, a behaviorist, author, and gifted storyteller, posted a poem on Facebook in January of 2024, and the poem went viral and moved many people. I am paraphrasing her beautiful story here in prose:

> At a crowded airport with cancelled flights, Christina was urgently trying to charge her phone to inform her son of her delay. Her attempt was interrupted by a woman who, in her own distress, slapped Christina's hand away from the shared charging port. This sudden aggression evoked a strong emotional response in Christina, who was ready to fight for that charging port.
>
> However, Christina's initial thoughts of retaliation quickly transformed into empathy. Recalling her father's wisdom about the futility of conflict, she offered to help the woman charge her phone instead. "Here, let me help you. Is it charging?" This act of kindness revealed the woman's own struggles: She was late, her young son was waiting alone, and her phone was nearly dead.

Subsequent tears and conversation created a bond over shared hardships and the realization that compassion was a simpler, more healing path than conflict. In this moment, an airport terminal became a place of human connection and understanding, reminding Christina of the power of empathy in transforming challenging situations.

"Love Is Easier" was the title of Christina's poem.

ELEVATION REQUIRES US TO RESTORE HOPE

To pull yourself out of the tension that exists in a moment of conflict, you have to believe that doing so will lead to a better result. And that requires hope: hope that a better outcome is possible.

This kind of hope is relatively easy to grab on to at a human scale, as revealed by the two stories I've told already in this chapter (my husband dealing with people cutting in line at the gas station, and Christina dealing with a woman who was rude at the airport). It is much harder to find when the scale is large and the conflict is the worst that humankind can envision.

Case in point: The aftermath of the events of October 7, 2023, when Hamas and other groups launched a surprise attack on Israel, is still playing out as I write this book. What has struck me most is the loss of trust I see around me, not just between the main players but the entire global audience that has a stake in the outcome. And while losing trust is scary and extremely sad, losing hope is far worse.

Immediately after the events of October 2023 in the Middle East, all I could think about was my family and friends in Israel and their immediate safety. I certainly didn't expect the instant tsunami of anti-Israel sentiments and activism that followed Israel's retaliation and bombardment of

Gaza. The world got sharply divided into opposing camps. I was and am devastated for both peoples, and it did not feel right picking sides. People were hurt and dying on both sides. People needed help, support, understanding, and empathy.

In a professional organization I belong to, EO (Entrepreneurs' Organization), two separate WhatsApp channels came alive. I immediately joined both and made sure to spend the same amount of time on each. I noticed how both channels were full of misinformation, fake news, unproven theories, and other news. And how both channels were being flooded with tears, sadness, frustration, helplessness, and anger.

It was clear that we needed to start a dialogue between these two groups, and in general between people with different perspectives on these events. I reached out to everyone I knew in the Middle East to enroll supporters and partners for this idea. I wanted to make sure I had enough people who supported different viewpoints who were willing to participate. Every one of my contacts said, "Yes, absolutely, we need to have a dialogue. But not now, it is too early, people are hurting too much." Basically, no for now.

But things were getting worse, not better. The situation was becoming more terrifying and desperate. The peace talks were going nowhere.

Meanwhile, people on all sides were experiencing a kind of isolation. I heard from friends around the world how afraid they were for their families' safety. They felt isolated, marginalized, and misunderstood. I heard similar sentiments of despair and loss of trust from others. They believed the global community was letting them disappear, that they were on their own.

But there was some hope. Together with several other EO-ers, we formed a small forum of eight people willing to have a dialogue despite having high emotions and opposite points of view. We called it Hope. We agreed to meet for two hours every two weeks on video. We were all entrepreneurs and CEOs running our businesses, and all of us were actively involved in helping our communities deal with the crisis. We were lucky to have two incredible facilitators and mentors from our entrepreneur community willing to donate their time to moderate and guide us through this hard process. Jesús de la Garza and Brian Brault, both experienced coaches and guides in navigating life challenges and difficult conversations, moderated with grace and acumen.

Every session felt like open-heart surgery to me. It took all my energy and then some to focus for two hours on seven other people who were pouring their hearts out, sharing their deepest fears and their sadness, anger, and disappointment with incredible honesty and courage. I poured my heart out too. I shared how hard it was for me to participate in community dinners when all the discussions were centered on the pain and fears of one group, with no mention of the pain and deaths among the others. In fact, any kind of community gathering became hard for me. What I noticed was a lack of questioning of the facts and the acceptance of possible doubt about what had happened or was happening. Instead people readily agreed with each other for the sake of belonging or remaining a part of their community.

During one Hope meeting in December of 2023, one of the participants shared that each time we were supposed to meet, she felt very hesitant to join again. She didn't know if she could continue facing not only us, people with different points of view, but if she could continue facing her own emotions and fears that kept coming up during our sessions. Even though our sessions did give her hope, she felt she was drowning in anger, fear, and despair for her people. She was not sure she could keep putting herself in that situation.

When it was my turn to share, I made a request of her and other members. "Please know that every time I see the images and videos of people walking through the rubble, hungry, scared, carrying their kids and a few belongings, with uncertainty and fear in their eyes, I see myself and my family. I see my cousins and relatives walking there. I know this was us, Eastern European Jews, running from the pogroms in Tzarist Russia in the nineteenth century. I have heard stories of my father as a two-year-old boy running away with his mom to Siberia from Ukraine during the Nazi German occupation of Ukraine in 1942. His stories are so vivid in my imagination, it feels as if I were there. So please every time you feel despair and loss of hope, remember that I know it could be us, it was us, and that I feel you and see you."

I received private messages from her later that night with gratitude for having met me. I felt the same about her. I felt as if I had found my sister. And I feel that our bond is strong, and it can survive disagreements, misunderstandings, hurt feelings, and conflicts as long as we keep nurturing it.

Since then, we've been able to meet in person. The first hug we shared felt like we had known each other all along, as if we had grown up together. We stay in touch through voice messages, we follow and support each other on social media, and in general hold each other close in our minds and hearts, supporting and loving from afar. We live far from each other, our lives are very different, and yet our bond keeps strengthening and expanding. This is the power of creating and giving hope to each other, especially under dire circumstances when we feel anger, fear, and despair, and where conflict is unavoidable and hope is hard to find. Helping each other find and nurture hope develops the type of deep closeness and connection, such a strong human bond, that is difficult to break.

HOPE IS THE ENGINE OF ELEVATION

I hear stories of hope overcoming conflict and despair every day. It's there if you choose it. On much larger scales, Hope and other stories you'll read about in this book continue to give me an extraordinary chance to experience the positive effects of letting collaboration lead the dance with conflict. Finding and nurturing hope together is about actively engaging in the hard work of staying curious, open-minded, and compassionate, even when the world around us is fragmented and divided. By sharing and keeping hope alive, we keep reminding each other to listen, to question assumptions, to postpone judgments, and to hold on to the shared humanity that connects us all.

Together we are able to create a space where recognizing the nature of our conflict creates the opportunity for real, authentic connection. Through this shared journey, we can find strength in our purpose and a deep sense of belonging that drives us forward, even in the face of uncertainty. In this space, hope becomes our anchor. And this is where true unity and peace have a chance to take root.

Chapter 2

IS IT POSSIBLE MY UNDERSTANDING IS FLAWED?

In pursuit of intellectual humility

Jonathan Haidt, a social psychologist, talks about how our moral beliefs are shaped less by logic and more by gut feelings, what he calls "moral intuitions." In *The Righteous Mind*, he describes how people from different political or cultural groups prioritize different moral foundations. For example, I once had a conversation with someone who was strongly opposed to immigration policies I supported. Initially, it felt impossible to connect. But when I asked why it mattered so much to him, he shared how his grandfather's job had been displaced years ago. For him, loyalty to family and to local community was core. That moment shifted the conversation from confrontation to collaboration. Haidt reminds us that when we understand someone's moral roots, we can speak to what matters most to them, not just argue from our own logic.

This kind of understanding doesn't come from debating harder. It comes from pausing long enough to ask, "What do I *not* understand here?" And that requires intellectual humility: the ability to acknowledge that our knowledge is incomplete or even flawed.

ASKING QUESTIONS VS. MAKING JUDGMENTS

The journey through conflict to collaboration is not only about perfecting our presence, but also about being willing to dismantle the mental walls we've built. Each assumption we hold is like a lens that distorts our view of others, narrowing our ability to see their full humanity. What happens when we dare to look beyond these lenses? What worlds might open up if we approach each encounter with radical curiosity instead of predetermined certainty? This is where our real work begins, in being brave enough to question everything we think we know.

Researcher Eranda Jayawickreme found that people who acknowledge they might be wrong are more open to learning from those they disagree with. In my own work, I've seen this play out. One workshop participant, a CEO of a high-tech startup from Seattle, admitted during a heated discussion, "I might be missing something here." That one sentence shifted the room. Instead of defending positions, others leaned in with questions. It wasn't about being right. It was about staying connected while still holding different truths.

In a world that often rewards certainty and speed, choosing humility and curiosity is an act of quiet rebellion. It doesn't mean giving up what we believe. It means holding our beliefs with open hands, willing to be surprised by someone else's truth.

Even though intellectual humility and empathy are powerful tools, overcoming deep-seated biases and entrenched views remains incredibly challenging, as we can all witness in our own lives daily. It's not easy, is it?

Eranda Jayawickreme points out that fostering intellectual humility requires a long-term commitment and systemic changes in education to teach critical thinking and openness to new perspectives.

And of course, there are limitations to what dialogues can achieve. Dialogues like those in Hope, which I discussed in the previous chapter, are invaluable for building personal connections, but they might not be enough to change the bigger structural and political issues that underpin these conflicts.

Jonathan Haidt points out that real change needs bigger efforts than just individual conversations. We're talking policy changes, education reforms, dealing with economic inequalities. Groups like the International Crisis Group say the same thing. We need cooperation and intervention to tackle deep conflicts that have been brewing for years.

So, while our heartfelt conversations and connections are essential, we also need to recognize that without bigger systemic changes it will be difficult to bridge these deep divides.

THE DANGER OF FALSE STORIES

We all make up stories. It's how our brains work: They fill in the blanks when we don't have all the facts. Sometimes, mental narratives are harmless, but often, the stories we invent can spiral into anxiety, misunderstandings, and unnecessary tension.

Making up stories often starts with small, everyday situations. For me, it happens when there's a gap between what I know and what I don't know. My brain rushes to fill that gap, and it doesn't always choose the most optimistic interpretation. Instead, it leaps to worst-case scenarios, as the following story shows.

My husband and I were swimming together far from shore while our three children were quietly playing and reading on Fanari Beach in Antiparos, Greece. It had been a trip full of activities but also one of disconnection for us as a couple. Jerome had spent most of the days kitesurfing, while I stayed on the beach reading and playing with the kids. Finally, we had this moment alone in the sea. But we came into it with very different expectations. Jerome wanted to swim peacefully, connecting through the act of swimming together, while I wanted to discuss an important and potentially fraught impending situation. I felt this was my chance to talk, and I didn't want to postpone what was on my mind.

It wasn't surprising that the conversation didn't go well. I was craving connection, but instead of explaining what I needed clearly, I launched into the topic. Jerome was confused and annoyed. He didn't understand why I was pushing this issue now when we were finally enjoying the sea together. The argument started quickly:

"Okay, then! Never mind!" I shouted.

"Fine," Jerome answered back.

I felt the sting of his tone, and I snapped back. What followed was one of those rare moments where both of us were frustrated, out of sync, and unable to see each other's needs. Suddenly, Jerome disappeared from view. I looked around, but I couldn't see him anywhere. My mind immediately filled in the blanks: Did he have a heart attack and drown? Did he just swim away, angry with me? What if something terrible happened?

I panicked. I am not a great swimmer, having only learned in my late thirties, and being far from the shore always feels a little unsafe for me. My fears about the deep water added to the storm of emotions. I tried to dive and look for him, but I couldn't see the bottom, which only made me more upset. What do I do? Do I swim to shore for help? How do I remember exactly where we were so I can point out the spot to rescuers? What will happen to our kids if something happens to him?

I swam toward the shore, my survival instinct kicking in. By the time I reached a place where I could stand and breathe, I saw Jerome swimming toward me from another direction. Relief flooded through me, followed quickly by anger: at him, at myself, at the fear that had taken over my mind.

When he reached me, he saw the fear and anger pouring out of me. Without asking questions, he hugged me as I cried. He didn't fully understand what had happened, but he knew I needed comfort, not explanations, in that moment.

The story of my husband's non-drowning has been one I've told over and over again, first to my children, then to my workshop audiences around the world, and even on my YouTube channel. Yes, my brain made up a story of my husband drowning instead of acknowledging that he told me he was going for a swim. Yes, I panicked when I believed that story. And yes, I am glad my survival instinct kicked in, and I didn't waste precious time waiting around.

These stories we invent can either disconnect us from reality or, when recognized, create pathways to deeper understanding. By learning to pause, to name these narratives, to check the facts, and to communicate openly, we begin practicing skills that allow us to embrace conflict as a learning experience. Allowing assumptions to rule our reactions is incompatible with intellectual humility.

The more I share this story, the less embarrassed I feel about my "great" ability to spin tales in my head. And the more I learn that I'm not alone in this. I've learned that when I have the intellectual humility to share this story of my imperfection, I find others reaching out with their own. These moments of *connection* remind me that it's okay to talk about this openly, and they create *collaboration* through shared vulnerability. We all need to be witnessed and seen, and we need to share strategies for how to handle these moments of mental storytelling. So, if this story resonated with you, please share your own.

Have you found yourself inventing scenarios or imagining intentions that weren't really there? Did you ever act out of those stories and see unintended consequences unfold? It's okay. Many of us do it. Talking about it and admitting that we made incorrect assumptions in our minds can help us grow and handle these situations better when they arise. As long as we do it with kindness to ourselves and without shame, we can improve the odds that collaboration through conflict will lead the tango, and that our relationships will stay healthy and supportive.

And again, this is a lesson that applies to larger scales as well. What my experience with Hope revealed goes far beyond this specific conflict. It showed me something fundamental about human collaboration: What keeps us apart isn't just our different backgrounds, experiences, or beliefs, it's the stories we make up about each other when understanding is missing. Even as we created space for different voices to express their truths, I recognized a pattern that extends into all our relationships. When someone's actions confuse us, or when we lack information, our minds instinctively fill those gaps with narratives of our own creation. I've come to see how these invented stories feed into conflict and become perhaps the most significant barriers to the connection we all desperately need.

Steps to Break the Cycle

I've learned that catching these invented stories takes practice. When I notice my mind spinning, I try to do three things:

- First, I name what's happening. I'll actually say to myself, "Wait, what story am I making up here?" In that moment in Greece, I could have thought, "I'm telling myself Jerome drowned. Is that really the only explanation?"

- Second, I check what I actually know. Jerome had told me he was going for a swim. I could have reminded myself of that fact instead of jumping to the worst conclusion.

- Third, I share what I'm feeling when I can. When Jerome reached me, I could have said, "I was so scared when I couldn't see you. I thought something terrible had happened." This creates space for real understanding.

THE POTENTIAL LONELINESS OF INTELLECTUAL HUMILITY

Practicing intellectual humility often means standing apart from our tribes. And that can feel profoundly lonely.

I had a big argument with my husband over whether we would participate in a demonstration organized in Paris called "Against Anti-Semitism." For me, this was yet another ritualized behavior of a group of people not being inclusive of other groups. I felt that adding "Against Islamophobia and Other Forms of Racism" would include more people and be more appropriate. So I didn't go with him.

Upon his return, I saw he was feeling reassured, renewed in his sense of belonging after the demonstration. It made me happy for him, but even more puzzled for me. *Where do I belong?*

We can all relate to how it feels not to belong. It's very uncomfortable. In fact, we know that belonging is one of the strongest components of a sense of well-being. It's especially uncomfortable not to belong at times of major conflicts. And yet here I was, on my own island full of doubt and uncertainty.

But I was also full of something else. I was full of the spirit of investigation and curiosity. Full of empathy for everyone who was suffering and afraid. And full of a sense of overwhelming hope. Hope that dialogue is still possible, if we're able to muster the effort, skill, and enough open hearts.

This is the paradox of intellectual humility. When we choose questioning over certainty, when we refuse to pick sides that feel too simple, when we insist on seeing the humanity in everyone, we often find ourselves alone. Our willingness to doubt our own understanding can leave us without a clear tribe to belong to.

The people who share our values might think we're not committed enough. The people who disagree with us might think we're still too far away. And sometimes, like me standing in my kitchen that evening in Paris, we're left wondering where exactly we fit.

But here's what I've discovered. This loneliness isn't a bug in the system. It's a feature. It's the space where real learning happens. It's where we develop the capacity to hold multiple perspectives without having to choose just one. It's where we practice the muscle of staying curious even when everyone around us has already decided what to think.

The loneliness of intellectual humility is temporary. The connections it makes possible? Those can last a lifetime.

When we're willing to sit with the discomfort of not belonging to any camp, we create space for people from all camps to find us. We become the bridge. We become the place where unlikely conversations can happen. We become proof that it's possible to care deeply about issues without losing our capacity to see and hear each other.

This doesn't mean abandoning our values. It means holding them with open hands. It means recognizing that our understanding is always incomplete, always evolving. It means choosing connection over correctness, even when, especially when, it leaves us standing alone for a while.

Have you ever found yourself in this space? Where your questions made you feel isolated from people you care about? Where your refusal to choose sides left you feeling like you didn't have a side at all?

If so, you're not alone in being alone. And you're practicing something important: the willingness to let your curiosity lead, even when it costs you comfort.

CELEBRATE DOUBT OVER CERTAINTY

It's only natural for us to seek and desire stability, and certainty provides a sense of security and predictability. Many of us fear the unknown and feel the discomfort that it brings. But feeling certainty can also create a false sense of control over life's outcomes, which is very attractive to hold on to.

Societal and cultural norms often push us toward certainty, celebrating those with clear answers and defined paths. From a young age, we are taught to seek and value clarity, whether through career goals, personal beliefs, or opinions on complex issues. Certainty is often equated with confidence and competence, while doubt can be misinterpreted as indecision or weakness.

Given these pressures, it's no wonder we often cling to certainty, even when it limits our ability to see other perspectives. Certainty feels safe; it offers the comfort of predictability in an unpredictable world. But this same safety can keep us from the growth and insights that come from questioning and exploring the unknown.

So how do we embrace uncertainty and doubt, then, with so much pressure to cling to certainty? Acknowledging that it encourages critical thinking and open-mindedness, and fosters resilience and adaptability, how do we develop practices and habits to nurture our ability to doubt productively?

Here are several of my touchstones:

- **Build a community of questioners.** Great value exists in discussing doubts and uncertainties with others. We can find comfort and support in a community that embraces questioning and celebrates uncertainty together.

- **Ask questions.** We need to constantly ask "why" and "how" if we want to dig deeper into topics. It's paramount not to accept things at face value but instead seek to understand underlying principles.

- **Seek diverse perspectives.** Engage with people who have different viewpoints and read widely from various sources to challenge our own perspectives. This supports the process of embracing doubt by challenging our certainties.

- **Embrace uncertainty.** Rather than simply acknowledging uncertainty, *actively embrace it* as a natural part of life. The Stoics teach us to focus on what we can control and release what we cannot, but this requires practice. Embracing uncertainty means finding strength in the unknown and using it as an opportunity for growth, rather than a source of fear. It's not just about tolerating uncertainty. It's about leaning into it, learning from it, and allowing it to expand our understanding and resilience.

- **Acknowledge and accept our own ignorance.** Ask "What can I learn from this?" whenever we are faced with new facts and opinions.

THE PAUSE THAT CHANGES EVERYTHING

You know that moment when you feel your face getting hot, your heart racing, maybe your hands starting to shake? That's your body telling you you're about to make a choice. You can either dive into the fight or find a way to step back and breathe.

I've learned something from watching my husband, Jerome, and from my own practice. In that split second when everything in you wants to react, there's usually a small space where you can pause. Not always, but often enough to make it worth trying.

Here's what I do when I catch myself in that moment. I take one slow breath and ask myself, "What do I need right now?" This question always opens me up to compassion toward myself, which then extends to the other person. Then I ask, "What happened to them? What am I missing here?"

If you're feeling brave, try this. Next time someone cuts in front of you or says something that makes your blood pressure spike or does that thing that always sets you off, see if you can find that pause. Maybe it's just one breath. Maybe it's lowering your voice instead of raising it. Maybe it's asking a question instead of making a statement.

I'm not asking you to become a saint overnight. I'm still working on this myself. But every once in a while, when I manage to choose connection over combat, something changes. They stop being so defensive. The whole conversation feels different. And I remember why this practice matters.

What would happen if, just once this week, you chose curiosity over certainty when someone triggered you? You don't have to give up your position. You just have to stay curious about theirs.

THE FIVE PRINCIPLES OF LOVING CONFLICT

	State	Step 1	Step 2	Step 3
PRINCIPLE 1 **Engage with Presence**	From Discomfort to Courage	Let's Get Real	You Are In Charge of You	Have a Cup of Tea

	State	Step 1	Step 2	Step 3
PRINCIPLE 2 **Assume Nothing**	From Close-Minded to Curious	There Is Enough	Notice It, Name It, Express It	We Are All Doing Our Best

	State	Step 1	Step 2	Step 3
PRINCIPLE 3 **Listen to Understand**	Moving from Distracted to Understanding	Start with Awareness	Don't Just Listen—Hear	No Solutions Required

	State	Step 1	Step 2	Step 3
PRINCIPLE 4 **The Art of Questioning**	From Defensive to Interested	Be Deliberate	Ask the Interested Question	Question Together

	State	Step 1	Step 2	Step 3
PRINCIPLE 5 **The Rule of Us**	From Divided to Connected	Pop the Bubble	Let's Play	It's Okay to Share

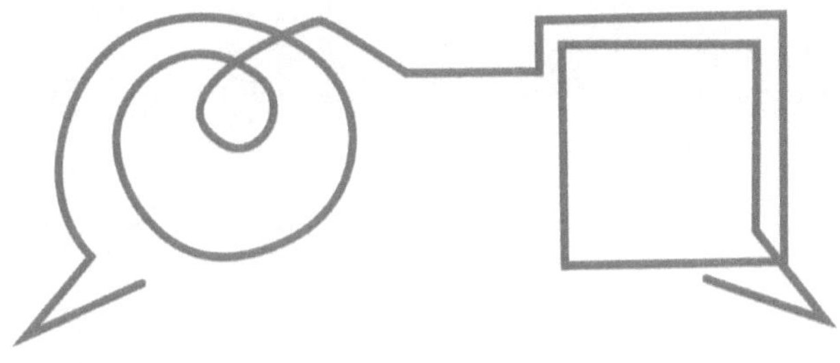

PART II

THE FIVE PRINCIPLES OF LOVING CONFLICT

THE FIVE PRINCIPLES OF LOVING CONFLICT

PRINCIPLE 1 Engage with Presence	PRINCIPLE 2 Assume Nothing	PRINCIPLE 3 Listen to Understand	PRINCIPLE 4 The Art of Questioning	PRINCIPLE 5 The Rule of Us

These five principles form our pathway to meaningful collaboration across differences:

- Engage with Presence, where we learn to move from discomfort to courage;

- Assume Nothing, where curiosity replaces our rush to judgment;

- Listen to Understand, where we go beyond hearing words to receiving the person;

- The Art of Questioning, where defensiveness gives way to genuine interest; and

- The Rule of Us, where division transforms into recognition of our shared humanity.

These principles aren't rigid steps to follow; they're movements in a dance that becomes more graceful with practice. They are a living, breathing approach to human interaction, calling for courage, persistence, vulnerability, and openness to transformation. Each principle builds upon the others, creating a continuous movement, much like an improvised dance of tango that taught me so profoundly about collaboration through conflict.

Throughout this part of the book, we'll explore each principle in depth, discovering how they work together to create authentic collaboration even across our deepest differences. You'll find stories from my own journey and others', practical tools to apply immediately, and reflections that invite you to see collaboration in a new light.

Reassurance: For Those Who Hate Conflict

If you picked up this book despite hating conflict, you're exactly who I wrote it for. I understand the physical discomfort of tension, the way your stomach drops when voices get raised, the exhaustion that comes from tiptoeing around difficult topics.

I know many of you might be here reluctantly. Maybe your spouse suggested this book. Maybe your business partner left it on your desk. In my workshops, people often tell me they hate conflict and would rather do anything else. I watch them sit in the back row, arms crossed, looking like they'd rather be getting a root canal.

But here's what I've discovered: The people who are most afraid of conflict often become the most skilled at having difficult conversations. Why? Because they're motivated to do it completely differently than what they experienced growing up.

After a "Loving Conflict" workshop in Seattle, a woman stayed behind to talk. "I've spent forty years avoiding conflict, and I can see I'm doing the same thing with my teenage daughter," she said. "I'm just realizing that all my avoiding was actually creating more problems."

A few months later, I heard from her. She mentioned that she and her daughter were talking more openly than they had in years. Not because they agreed on everything but because they'd learned they could disagree without it meaning the relationship was in danger.

What I'm offering isn't more conflict in your life. It's more skill in handling the conflicts that are already there. When you learn to love conflict, you transform the conflicts you can't avoid into opportunities for deeper collaboration.

Principle 1

ENGAGE WITH PRESENCE

*	State	Step 1	Step 2	Step 3
PRINCIPLE 1 **Engage with Presence**	From Discomfort to Courage	Let's Get Real	You Are In Charge of You	Have a Cup of Tea

From Discomfort to Courage

In my middle school back in Soviet Ukraine, a group of boys continually bullied a short, slight boy named Sasha who wore glasses. He was very smart, but shy and awkward, and he could not or would not defend himself. All the other students just stood back and watched him being beaten up.

So did I for a long time. I was eleven years old, scared of these boys, and wanted to fit in and behave like everyone else in the group. But I felt angry, devastated, and worthless. I wanted to help Sasha (like I always wanted to and still want to help and stand up for anyone who is being singled out, excluded, or unfairly treated) but did not know how.

One day they beat him bloody and then laughed at his tears. I thought, "There must be a way to stop this!"

No one ever tried to talk to those boys. They were shunned, rejected, isolated, and feared. There was a clear divide in the schoolyard: the A+ students and the kids who were our friends versus the strong boys who sat at the back of the classroom and didn't seem to care about failing school.

But I wanted to know who they were, where they came from, and why they were behaving this way. Maybe if I understood them, I could help them see me and eventually little Sasha. And maybe, just maybe, if they got to know him, would they stop the bullying?

I started talking to them, the only one from our group of A+ students to actually become curious about them and ask them questions. I first asked them if I could help them with their homework, and if they could help me with mine. I had to stretch the truth there, but at that young age I had an intuition about how connecting it can be to ask someone for help. So, I found questions and issues they could possibly help with.

Step by step, our connection developed. I went to their houses, met their parents, spent hours listening to heavy metal music that they were fans of, and watched them play soccer. I invited them to my house to study together and helped them with their homework.

And we talked. A lot. I asked them lots of questions about their lives. And told them about mine, until in the end, we became friends.

A whole new universe opened up for me. In many cases, their parents did not have many resources, or the father was an alcoholic who abused their mother regularly. Some could not study at home because it was not safe due to the abuse. But what I also discovered was that they were sensitive, street smart, and funny.

And as much as I learned from them, they learned from me. Those divides that were so entrenched on the schoolyard slowly but surely disappeared. It was no longer us versus them; we were all spending time together, the A+ students and the boys from the back of the classroom.

That's how they also got to know little Sasha. One day we included him in one of our games. The next day he got to help one of the boys with his homework. Sasha had all these opportunities to show who he was: a smart, witty, kind, and funny kid.

Most importantly, the boys stopped bullying Sasha. Because now instead of being someone they did not understand, he became someone they knew. They also stopped being isolated by others in school. They stayed in school until graduation, and we still keep in touch.

Facing that group of boys taught me many important lessons. I learned how to listen with curiosity and without judgment to someone who, at first glance, seemed very different from me. That's how they listened to me, even though I came from a very different cultural, social, and economic background. I did not feel judged by them, and they asked tons of questions and truly listened. So, I learned to listen like they did.

I got to practice courage. I was very scared to approach them that first time in the schoolyard. I was afraid they would laugh at me, dismiss me, ignore me, or beat me up. And yet I gathered the courage to start that first conversation, to step into the conflict. And the positive learning, deep connection, and inspiration I received from practicing this courage keeps on giving to me today: in my entrepreneurial life, in my travels, and in many challenging situations I have faced ever since.

I got to understand firsthand how circumstances can shape us. Their life was very different from mine, and as such, their behaviors, mindsets, and reactions were very different as well. While my family did everything possible to nurture and aid my studies, it often seemed like no one around them cared about theirs. While I had all the resources available to me to learn and practice what I was interested in, dance, music, languages, they had access to very little. In fact, the first time they came to my house and saw our gigantic library (my parents were always obsessed with reading) they were shocked and spent hours just looking through the books in awe and wonder. That moment was a pivotal moment for me when I started appreciating and being grateful for everything I had access to that others might not have, and how this access or the lack of it might change the trajectory of our lives.

I also learned what it meant to be street smart. They showed me the streets in ways I never saw them or ever imagined them to be. Since they spent much more time on the streets without supervision than I did, they knew their way around. They showed me how to be outside and watch out for my safety and the safety of others. This skill has served me well and keeps doing so on the streets of Paris, Shanghai, Caracas, or Buenos Aires. It has kept me safe in many difficult and even dangerous situations.

Of course, I would not have been able to learn any of their important life skills if I had not mustered up my courage to put the boys in a position to teach me. I truly saw them as my teachers and paid all the respect to them as I normally would to the teachers I trusted and admired. They must have felt it, and they paid me back manyfold.

I am sure you, too, have your own story about conflict or confrontation. How many times did you lean into these difficult situations, hard conversations, and conflicts? Or did you shy away from them? There are so many reasons we tell ourselves to *not* engage in a conflict. But what we forget is that these are such valuable moments in our lives. Moments of courage and major opportunities for growth and collaboration.

So, you probably know from experience this simple truth: Only by going into conflict and facing confrontation can we bridge division and disconnection, personal, professional, societal, cultural. In fact, this is the only way for change, understanding, and creativity. It is *through* the conflict.

Conflict can be internal or external. It might be a conflict with yourself. For example, maybe you want to present in front of a big audience but are facing the discomfort of impostor syndrome so many of us carry. It might be a conflict with a parent who is a strong believer in a different political party from you. It might be a conflict with your CEO, manager, or colleague with whom you completely disagree on the company strategy. It might be a conflict with another country that has an entirely different culture from yours.

A willingness to embrace and move beyond discomfort in the face of conflict is the starting point of engaging with presence. What it takes to do that is the subject of the rest of this chapter.

STEPPING INTO DISCOMFORT

All these conflict situations are extremely uncomfortable and can have devastating and even violent outcomes. I am sure some of you felt physical discomfort just now when you were reading these lines. You might have felt tightness in your chest, shortness of breath, rigidity in your muscles, discomfort in your stomach, or the hint of a headache.

These reactions are normal when you are faced with someone drastically different from you and the potential for conflict is high. The tightness in your chest when a colleague expresses a worldview that feels alien to yours. The subtle withdrawal when a family member triggers old wounds. The barely perceptible tension when encountering someone from a culture you don't understand.

Even after decades of loving conflict and practicing connection and collaboration, I experience these physical responses. My heart races, my mouth goes dry, and every instinct tells me to retreat. These are the moments when collaboration feels most impossible. Yet paradoxically, these are precisely the moments when the opportunity for meaningful connection is greatest, if only we can get past the assumptions and judgments that arise automatically.

This is what *engaging with presence* means to me. It's about stepping into that discomfort rather than away from it. It's about being fully here, in this moment, with this person, however different they may seem. I've learned this lesson through both triumph and failure, where cultural differences kept people from hearing each other, at family gatherings where political divides threatened to sever relationships, and in countless interactions where the prospect of collaboration felt both thrilling and terrifying.

What I've discovered is this: When we engage with presence, even the most challenging conversations become opportunities. Not to change minds or win arguments but to understand and be understood. To remember our shared humanity beneath our differences. To find, perhaps, an unlikely ally where we least expected one.

LOVING CONFLICT ENOUGH TO STAY ENGAGED

In Hong Kong, I worked with a family business where three generations were locked in what felt like permanent disagreement about the company's direction. The grandfather wanted traditional approaches, the father pushed for moderate innovation, and the daughter advocated for complete digital transformation.

During our "Loving Conflict" session, I asked them to practice staying present with each other's concerns instead of immediately defending their positions. What emerged surprised everyone. The grandfather wasn't actually opposed to change. He was terrified of losing the relation-ships that had built the business. The daughter wasn't trying to destroy tradition. She was afraid the company would become irrelevant and the family legacy would disappear.

By the end of that four-hour workshop, they had created a transi-tion plan that honored the grandfather's relationships, incorporated the father's steady approach, and implemented the daughter's digital vision. Six months later, the company had its strongest quarter in five years.

This is what becomes possible when we love conflict enough to stay present with it instead of trying to win it.

HOW TO ENGAGE WITH PRESENCE

Engaging with presence is the foundation of all learning to love con-flict. Without being fully in the moment, grounded in reality rather than reaction, none of the principles that follow can take root. This principle requires both courage and vulnerability: the courage to face discomfort and the vulnerability to be truly seen.

Over the past twenty-five years, I have distilled engaging with presence into three simple steps that you'll read about in the next chapters:

*	State	Step 1	Step 2	Step 3
PRINCIPLE 1 **Engage with** **Presence**	From Discomfort to Courage	Let's Get Real	You Are In Charge of You	Have a Cup of Tea

- **Step 1: Let's get real.** See what's actually happening around us rather than what we fear or assume.

- **Step 2: You are in charge of you.** Master your emotions, not by suppressing them but by recognizing them as messengers; control emotions so they don't escalate conflict or get in the way of connection and presence.

- **Step 3: Have a cup of tea.** Slow down and create a shared pause, a metaphorical "cup of tea" that allows you to maneuver through conflict.

The practice of engaging with presence transforms how we connect with others across differences. By getting real about what's actually happening rather than what we assume, mastering our emotional responses rather than being driven by them, and creating deliberate space for collaboration, we develop the courage to stay present even when faced with actual or potential conflict and when discomfort arises.

Although practicing these movements can initially feel unfamiliar, we're all learning together. Sometimes I catch myself making assumptions or reacting before choosing my response, but each attempt builds our capacity for presence. So don't feel discouraged if these steps do not come naturally to you at first. In the next three chapters, I'll walk through each of the steps and provide background, tips, and specific actions you can take to master that step.

Step 1

LET'S GET REAL

	State	Step 1	Step 2	Step 3
PRINCIPLE 1 Engage with Presence	From Discomfort to Courage	Let's Get Real	You Are In Charge of You	Have a Cup of Tea

Born in Chicago in 1958, Daryl Davis encountered the harshness of racism as a ten-year-old Black Cub Scout. While marching with his troop, rocks were hurled at him by onlookers, a brutal expression of prejudice. Fortunately, this didn't embitter him. Instead, it inspired a profound question that, based on Davis's testimonials, would shape his life: Why would people hate me without knowing me?

Fast forward to 1983, when Davis performed as a pianist at the Silver Dollar Lounge in Maryland. After his set, an older White man approached him, marveling at his talent and comparing him to Jerry Lee Lewis. When Davis explained that Lewis's style was influenced by Black musicians, the man was surprised.

What began as an innocent musical debate quickly turned into something extraordinary. The man revealed something that stunned Davis. He was a member of the Ku Klux Klan. As Davis described it later, this man admitted that he had never shared a drink or a conversation with a Black man before. Yet here he was, sitting with Davis, laughing and marveling over music.

The exchange didn't stop at pleasantries. Davis, fueled by curiosity rather than judgment, asked the man questions. He wanted to understand the roots of the man's beliefs. The Klansman answered candidly, explaining his worldview. And in that moment, Davis saw something unexpected. A crack in the wall that fear and hatred had built. It was the start of an extraordinary journey.

What made this interaction so remarkable was Davis's approach. Instead of confronting the man with anger or dismissing him outright, Davis leaned into the discomfort. He listened, genuinely and without judgment. He asked questions, not to prove the man wrong, but to understand him better.

By the end of their conversation, they were not enemies. They were, surprisingly, something closer to friends. Despite their stark differences, they found a connection through music and dialogue.

That night marked the beginning of Davis's extraordinary journey. Over the years, his patient, nonjudgmental approach to these conversations inspired over two hundred Klansmen to leave the Klan, many giving him their robes as a symbol of change. It was a powerful reminder that even the deepest divides can sometimes be bridged through understanding and genuine human connection. His approach was slow and deliberate, built on a foundation of face-to-face conversations, mutual respect, and an unshakable commitment to understanding.

One of the most powerful examples of this approach is his relationship with Roger Kelly, a Grand Dragon of the KKK in Maryland. Their story began through an introduction by a mutual friend who believed Davis might have a chance to connect with Kelly. The first meeting took place in a hotel room, a neutral, albeit tense, space where both men were surrounded by supporters. Kelly, accompanied by his armed bodyguard, exuded authority and caution, while Davis, armed only with his questions and calm demeanor, sought to break through the layers of prejudice.

From the very beginning, Davis made it clear that he was not there to confront Kelly but to understand him. He asked open-ended questions: How can you hate me without knowing me? What do you believe, and why? These questions were not rhetorical; Davis genuinely wanted to hear Kelly's answers. In turn, Kelly was taken aback by Davis's approach. He had encountered anger and confrontation before, but never such a genuine curiosity about his beliefs.

These meetings were not one-offs. Davis and Kelly met repeatedly over the years, in homes, public places, and other neutral venues. The conversations often started cautiously, but as Davis continued to listen and engage without judgment, Kelly began to lower his defenses. He started questioning the very ideology that had defined his identity for so long.

As their relationship deepened, Davis didn't shy away from expressing the pain and harm caused by the KKK's beliefs and actions. However, he always did so with composure and respect, ensuring the conversations remained dialogues rather than debates. Over time, Kelly began to see Davis not as an enemy, but as a friend. This shift culminated in a powerful gesture: Kelly left the Klan, handing Davis his Grand Dragon robe as a symbol of his transformation.

The bond between the two grew so strong that Kelly asked Davis to be the godfather of his granddaughter. This remarkable evolution, from wary strangers on opposites sides of race conflict to trusted friends, stands as a testament to the power of getting real, of not letting assumptions or prior beliefs stand in the way of collaboration.

Davis's story shows the first step in falling in love with conflict is to ground ourselves in reality. We must learn to see situations as they truly are, not as we fear them to be or wish them to be. This is where our journey of engagement truly begins: with getting real. This lets us see situations clearly rather than through the distorted lens of our assumptions or fears. When we get real, we create the foundation for authentic collaboration by starting with what actually is, not what we imagine.

The challenge is that when in a conflict, we almost always assume negative things about our opponent, which leads us to be defensive, closed off, and ready to go into battle instead of being ready to learn. To change our assumptions, we need to get real by asking ourselves *what's real* about the situation, *what's real* about the other person, and *what's real* about ourselves. These questions can shift us out of conflict mode and into an open, fact-finding mindset. Let's explore how to become conscious of your assumptions and open yourself to reality.

INTELLECTUAL HUMILITY: THE FOUNDATION OF GETTING REAL

I love how Winston Churchill put it: "In the course of my life, I have often had to eat my words, and I must confess that I have always found it a wholesome diet." Doesn't that capture it perfectly? There's something surprisingly nourishing about admitting we got something wrong.

I've had to eat my own words many times. Like when I was convinced my approach to business negotiations was the only way, until my Chinese partners showed me an entirely different path that worked better. Or when I was so sure I understood why someone acted a certain way, only to discover I'd completely misread the situation. These moments of realizing I was wrong haven't diminished me. They've expanded my world and connected me with people I might otherwise never have understood.

That's why I consider intellectual humility to be the foundation of getting real. This recognition that maybe, just maybe, I don't have all the answers. It's that voice that whispers, "What if I'm missing something here?" even when I feel absolutely certain.

When we acknowledge that we don't have all the answers, several things happen:

We become open to new information. Letting go of the idea that we know everything allows us to see the world with fresh eyes. It helps us absorb new ideas and perspectives that we might have dismissed before. This openness can lead to exciting shifts in our understanding and better decisions. It's like saying out loud, "I'm ready to learn something new," and meaning it.

We approach conflicts with curiosity, not defensiveness. Conflicts feel less threatening when we admit we might not have the whole picture. Instead of seeing disagreements as battles to win, we can approach them as opportunities to ask questions and explore. This changes the dynamic from "me versus you" to "let's figure this out together."

We build stronger relationships. When we show others that we value their perspectives, we create trust and respect. People feel more connected to us when they know we're listening and willing to consider their views. This kind of humility can strengthen both personal and professional relationships, reminding us that collaboration works better than always needing to be right.

We grow, intellectually and emotionally. Being humble about what we don't know keeps us growing. It makes learning exciting rather than intimidating. At the same time, it helps us face mistakes or new insights without feeling defensive. Admitting we're works in progress is freeing; it reminds us we don't have to have it all figured out, and that's okay.

USING HUMAN QUALITIES TO GET REAL: THE DARYL DAVIS METHOD

Daryl Davis's method was not about winning arguments. It was and is about showing respect, building trust, and creating a space where individuals can question their own beliefs. His superpowers, which were bravery, openness, curiosity, and active listening, allowed him to achieve what many would deem impossible: turning enemies into friends.

For Davis, these interactions are not just personal victories. One of his best-known quotes is: "Ignorance breeds fear, fear breeds hatred, and hatred breeds destruction." Through education and connection, Davis believes ignorance can be dismantled and understanding can flourish even in the face of conflict. Davis didn't set out to change minds through arguments or confrontation. Instead, he relied on a set of deeply human qualities:

- **Bravery:** willingly entering spaces where he was unwelcome

- **Openness and curiosity:** seeking to understand opposing viewpoints without immediate judgment

- **Respect and genuine interest:** valuing individuals as human beings beyond their affiliations

- **Active listening:** allowing others to express their beliefs fully before responding

- **Patiently challenging views:** encouraging self-reflection through thoughtful questioning

In his book *Klan-destine Relationships* and the documentary *Accidental Courtesy*, Davis shares these powerful stories, along with the challenges he faced, not only from Klansmen but also from critics within his own community.

When I first heard Davis's story, I immediately wished it would be possible for me to know him, to be his friend. To be able to witness his journey of connecting with people so starkly different from himself would mean seeing the potential for reconciliation and understanding in even the most divided spaces. I often return to his story when I feel unsettled or disheartened by hostility and division. His life reminds me that the path to change begins with a conversation, a brave, honest, and open conversation.

Davis's story challenges us to confront our own biases, to extend a hand to those we might fear or misunderstand, and to see the humanity in everyone. He chose engagement over avoidance, conversation over conflict. His life shows us that it's possible to bridge divides, even the deepest ones, and that the journey toward dismantling hate begins with the simple act of listening.

Thank you, Daryl Davis, for showing us the way and inspiring us to engage with courage, respect, and hope.

TOOLS FOR GETTING REAL

There are a number of tools and techniques for helping us get real. I'll talk about them next, but first let me relate a story that I'll use to show how the tools work.

> My friend Claude was driving in heavy traffic in Paris. He was late after work, irritated, and tired, and couldn't wait to get home. He was in his car, inching ever so slowly in an almost stand-still traffic jam. Finally, he reached a place where two lanes were merging. The rule in France is that drivers take turns to merge. Claude sat there, waiting for his turn.
>
> Finally, it was his turn to merge into the road. However, the car next to him kept moving forward, pushing its way

through. Claude was furious and getting more so. "What kind of person does that?" he thought. He did what many of us would do in a similar situation. He didn't make eye contact with the other driver and kept trying to merge, growing angrier by the second.

When there was finally no more space between two cars, he looked up to see the other driver. To his great surprise, what he saw was not another angry face. Instead, he was met with a pleading look on the other driver's face:

"I'm so sorry, I'm being towed!"

Tool 1. Byron Katie's Four Questions

I first learned about this process of investigation from Byron Katie, who's like the Sherlock Holmes of thinking. She helps us investigate what's real versus what's just our mind playing tricks on us. Katie suggests we ask ourselves four questions when we're convinced the person in front of us is the villain of our story:

- **Is it true?** For example, if we were Claude, could we be sure the other driver is an inconsiderate road hog or could they just be having a really bad day?

- **Can we absolutely know what's true?** Unless we're mind readers, we can't really know what's going on in the other driver's mind.

- **How do we react when we believe we know the truth?** Maybe, like Claude, we're ready to descend into Parisian (or any other city's) road rage.

- **Who would we be without that thought?** Perhaps we'd be someone enjoying a peaceful, even if slow, drive while listening to some relaxing music.

Byron Katie's method acts as a mental pause button, giving us a chance to step back from instant reactions and see stressful situations in a more analytical light, with a little less drama and a bit more humor about ourselves and our story-making minds.

Tool 2. Understand Your Mind's (Bad) Shortcuts: Your Cognitive Biases

What often lead us astray during potential conflicts are what is known as cognitive biases. These are mental shortcuts that distort our view of reality, pulling us toward misunderstandings instead of clarity.

- **Confirmation Bias** is like our brain putting on its own rose-colored glasses, making us see only what we want to see. In conflicts, this means we focus on details that support our viewpoint while conveniently ignoring those that don't. For Claude, this bias made him assume the other driver was simply being rude, reinforcing his frustration.

- **Fundamental Attribution Error Bias** makes us lenient judges of our own actions but harsh critics of others. When someone cuts us off in traffic, we think, "What a rude driver!" But when we do it, we excuse ourselves: "Oh, that was just a simple mistake." Claude assumed the worst about the driver's character instead of considering other explanations.

- **Negativity Bias** makes our minds latch onto the negative, which serves to amplify conflict. Claude's mind darkened his interpretation of the driver's actions, fueling his anger instead of allowing space for understanding.

HOW TO USE THIS KNOWLEDGE: THE BIAS CHECK METHOD

Now that you know these biases exist, here's how to catch them in action during conflicts:

When you feel that familiar surge of frustration or anger, stop. Take one deep breath and ask yourself: "What story am I telling myself right now?" This simple pause creates the space needed to examine your thinking.

Then ask yourself these three questions:

- **Confirmation Bias Check:** What evidence am I ignoring that doesn't fit my story?

- **Attribution Error Check:** If I did the exact same thing, how would I explain it?

- **Negativity Bias Check:** Am I assuming the worst possible interpretation here?

With these questions answered, generate at least two other explanations for what happened. For Claude's situation: Maybe the driver was rushing to the hospital. Maybe they genuinely didn't see him. Maybe they misjudged the distance.

Now you can respond from curiosity rather than certainty. Instead of anger driving your actions, understanding becomes possible. This method doesn't eliminate biases; they're hardwired into us. But it gives you the power to recognize them before they hijack your response and turn a minor misunderstanding into a major conflict.

Tool 3. Engage "System 2" Thinking

Psychologists Daniel Kahneman and Amos Tversky, in their book *Thinking, Fast and Slow*, describe two systems of thought:

- **System 1** is quick, instinctive, and emotional, reacting on gut feelings and often letting biases lead the way.
- **System 2** is slow, deliberate, and logical, taking time to sift through facts and consider alternative perspectives.

When Claude told me the story of what he initially thought was an inconsiderate driver, the impact on him was palpable. He looked shocked, amazed, embarrassed, and inspired by the shift he experienced. He said it changed his behavior, and he now always checks what's real before reacting. His initial reaction, anger and assuming, was driven by System 1. However, when he saw the apologetic look on the driver's face, it activated System 2. He realized he had been impatient and angry because he assumed negative things about the other person. He hadn't paused to check what was real. He hadn't considered an alternative to what he thought was happening.

If he had paused earlier to ask himself "What's real here?" or "Is there more to this picture?" he might have been able to bypass his biases and approach the situation with more curiosity and less judgment.

Tool 4. The Scientific Method as a Tool for Reality-Checking

Most of us learned about the scientific method in school. What I've discovered is that this same approach can help us move through conflicts. When emotions run high and I'm making assumptions about someone's behavior, I can use these same steps to check what's actually real. Not only the scientists among us can benefit from its everyday use.

For example, in Claude's situation, the method would provide a means for analyzing the situation in a productive way:

1. **Observation:** Traffic was heavy, and the other car didn't let him merge.

2. **Question Formulation:** Why isn't this driver letting me in?

3. **Hypothesis Development:** Perhaps they're rude and inconsiderate.

4. **Experimentation:** Instead of reacting angrily, check for other possibilities (e.g., look at the driver's face).

5. **Data Analysis:** The driver's apologetic look and the towing situation revealed a different truth.

By pausing and engaging a more deliberate process like the scientific method, we can navigate conflicts with greater clarity and objectivity.

WHY GETTING REAL MATTERS

Equipping ourselves with facts instead of assumptions can dissolve defensiveness, anger, and closed-mindedness. The process of gathering information calls on our inner scientist to investigate and get to the facts, making the process of conflict resolution more interesting. It may even help us to love it (or at least like it) more.

Step 2

YOU ARE IN CHARGE OF YOU

	State	Step 1	Step 2	Step 3
PRINCIPLE 1 Engage with Presence	From Discomfort to Courage	Let's Get Real	You Are In Charge of You	Have a Cup of Tea

As I sit down to write today, the sounds of my household are very present. I hear my mother patiently reading to my nine-year-old daughter a book in Ukrainian that has been read and reread many times, and she knows it by heart. I see my father playing chess with my twelve-year-old son, carefully explaining to him why following the rules can be useful, and taking this conversation deeper and wider into the philosophy of life as he always does.

The sounds of my household serve as a constant reminder of the journey I am on. Living at this unique crossroads, where my original Ukrainian and Jewish culture intertwine with the ones I adopted along the way, Chinese and American, and the French one I am now surrounded by, has its own set of challenges. It is a daily dance of juggling different cultural preferences, personal triggers, and geopolitical sensitivities, all while living and working with people from across the globe. Each day brings with it a kaleidoscope of emotions and interactions that test my resolve in mastering my emotions.

In this vibrant and often chaotic environment, emotional mastery is not just a theoretical concept. It is a necessary tool for survival and connection.

There are moments when my parents say something, and I am sent back to my five-year-old state of mind, blood rushing to my face; stubbornness and anger rule. Or when the cultural nuances I encounter at my husband's French family gathering fiercely clash with my own. Or when a simple misunderstanding with a colleague from another part of the world reminds me of the intricate web of human emotions and perceptions. Or when a geopolitical situation (like the war in Ukraine and China siding with Russia, the aggressor) brings up huge emotions in the otherwise rational business conversation between my business partners from these parts of the world.

It's in these moments that I realize mastering my emotions is more than just personal work, it's a bridge to understanding and connecting with others in a world that's increasingly interconnected yet diversely complex.

Through practicing emotional mastery, I discovered that to reach out to others, I first need to be in charge of myself. By creating that vital space between stimulus and response, I've found a path to more meaningful collaborations across cultures, generations, and differences. Each day brings new opportunities to practice this essential skill: a skill that doesn't just change our interactions but transforms who we become in the process.

When we master our emotions, we gain the ability to recognize what truly matters to us and open ourselves to understanding what truly matters to others. That's the essence of the phrase "You are in charge of you."

ANGER ILLUMINATES VALUES

While it's important to control all our emotions when trying to connect with others, especially those who are outwardly different from ourselves, it's anger that demands the most attention because it can derail our efforts. That said, I learned a piece of wisdom early on while doing business in China: "Show me your anger, and I will tell you who you are."

My first business was a brand-management agency I set up in Shanghai, China, with the ambitious goal of opening China's market to top American and European brands. My company's first client was Church's Chicken, a fried chicken franchise that followed KFC's significant success in the Chinese market. They hired us to build a franchising network, which included finding the right franchisees, managing relationships, and building a supply chain for equipment. But our main role was serving as a bridge between two very different cultures: American and Chinese.

The negotiations between the American team and Mr. Zhang, a successful restaurateur in Shanghai, were tense. The Americans wanted everything spelled out in the contract, while the Chinese side viewed the contract as just the beginning, a framework to be renegotiated as the relationship evolved. The cultural differences were stark, and tensions were high.

At one point, Tom Johnson, the American executive, a seasoned, globally experienced businessman, lost his temper. He raised his voice and hit the table with his fist. The room fell silent. All eyes were on Mr. Zhang. But Mr. Zhang did not react at all. He just sat there. Calmly. Watching Tom. Chinese people learn to master their emotions from an early age. It is not at all about "controlling" their emotions or not letting them be seen. It is rather about recognizing them, and expressing them when and how it is appropriate for the particular situation. I was exposed to this when I began working with Chinese people, and I am still learning and perfecting this craft.

Mr. Zhang later explained to me that he was thrilled he got to watch Tom get angry and lose his temper. He needed to go through the conflict with the potential partner to see how that partner would behave. He said, "If they show their anger, that means they care about this project. If they care, so will I. I love conflicts for the learnings they bring us."

Luckily it was time for lunch, and Mr. Zhang hosted us in one of his restaurants that specialized in Shanghai cuisine. That's when the pivotal moment of this partnership occurred. Mr. Zhang was explaining the intricacies of each dish, the combination of spices, and what cookware and cooking skills were necessary to achieve this level of excellence. Tom listened and watched Mr. Zhang. He understood and felt the passion Mr. Zhang had for the food industry. This was the "cup of tea" moment when passions were revealed; it was the link of common humanity moment. Both Mr. Zhang and Tom were able to relax, breathe, and think clearly.

We signed the agreement shortly after lunch.

Simon Sinek once expressed a similar sentiment about anger during his podcast interview with Brené Brown and Adam Grant, saying, "When was the last time you got angry? Tell me, and I will tell you what your values are."

Both the Chinese statement and Sinek's version reflect the same core idea: Anger is often a window into what we value most. It reveals the lines we cannot tolerate being crossed, the beliefs we hold dearest, and the moments where we feel our integrity is most challenged. If we think back to moments when we witness other people in anger, or the moments when we've been angry, we're very likely to come face-to-face with what we really care about.

In *The Dance of Anger*, Dr. Harriet Lerner discusses how anger can be a signal that something is wrong and needs attention. She states: "Anger is a tool for change when it challenges us to become more of an expert on the self and less of an expert on others."

THE UNIVERSALITY OF ANGER

Even if we recognize the value of anger in revealing priorities, many of us shy away from this emotion. We're taught to hide or suppress our anger, and witnessing it in others makes us uncomfortable.

How we express anger varies dramatically. Western cultures often encourage open expressions of anger as assertiveness. Eastern cultures like Japan tend to suppress it to maintain harmony. In Greece or Italy, anger is displayed more passionately but still seen as potentially disruptive.

Indigenous and African cultures often channel anger through storytelling or communal practices. The Navajo Talking Circle transforms personal anger into collective wisdom. South African Xhosa traditions express anger as stories about community impact rather than individual blame.

Across all cultures, though, one thing is clear: Anger makes people uncomfortable. It's viewed as chaotic, unpredictable, even dangerous. This discomfort drives us to suppress or avoid it, missing the opportunity to see it for what it really is: a window into our deepest values.

TOOLS OF EMOTIONAL MASTERY

I decided to focus on anger early in this chapter because it is a strong emotion that is universally shared. But the tools needed to deal with anger are the same as for any other strong emotion. And that's the key. Understanding our emotions is one thing; choosing how to respond to them is another. Our ability to elevate above our initial reactions and choose a response that aligns with our deeper values and goals for collaboration is where true emotional mastery shows up.

One basic skill is learning to use "I" statements. For example, saying, "I feel frustrated because I . . ." focuses on personal experience rather than blaming the other person. This approach not only helps to de-escalate conflicts but also invites the other person to take the time to truly hear what matters to you. Blame, on the other hand, often triggers defensiveness, shutting down meaningful dialogue. Boundaries also play a crucial role in managing anger. Articulating what is acceptable and what isn't, such as stating that personal attacks are off-limits, keeps the focus on the issue at hand. If those boundaries are crossed, it's important to calmly reinforce them or step away to regroup.

Tip: Practice with Your Family (But Be Gentle with Yourself)

A quote attributed to Ram Dass feels particularly relevant: "If you think you are enlightened, go and spend a week with your family."

He's right, because practicing emotional mastery with family is possibly the hardest place to start. Family knows exactly which buttons to push because they installed them. And those buttons often connect to stories and wounds that go back generations. This is why we need tremendous compassion for ourselves and for them. We're all carrying decades of history, sometimes centuries of patterns, into every conversation.

Even so, family gatherings like holiday dinners give us chances to practice. These settings often present challenges as well as opportunities, especially when navigating old patterns or sensitive dynamics. It's important to be gentle with ourselves, acknowledging that we will make mistakes, especially when dealing with family.

When emotions start to feel overwhelming and staying present becomes difficult, it can help to simply pause and say: "I'd like to keep talking, but I notice I'm getting overwhelmed. Could we take a short break, please?" This small but deliberate action can create space for both yourself and the other person, allowing for a calmer and more productive interaction.

Here are some other favorite techniques of mine for dealing with strong emotions.

Six Methods for Creating a Pause Between Stimulus and Reaction

Viktor Frankl, a Holocaust survivor, renowned Austrian psychiatrist, and the author of *Man's Search for Meaning*, is often credited with the following profound insight: "Between stimulus and response, there is a space. In that space is our power to choose our response. In our response lies our growth and freedom."

Expanding this space is the essence of emotional mastery. Mindfulness practices such as meditation, yoga, and mindful breathing help us cultivate this ability over time.

But what about those high-emotion moments when we need immediate tools?

We all face moments when emotions threaten to overtake our rational thinking. Maybe you've experienced that surge of anger when a colleague takes credit for your work during an important presentation, and you feel your face flush and hands tremble. Or perhaps you've felt that knot in your stomach when a family member makes a passive-aggressive comment at a holiday dinner, triggering old patterns and tensions that have existed for decades.

Then there are those high-stakes business situations, the negotiation where millions hang in the balance, when the other party suddenly makes an unreasonable demand and you feel your heart racing, knowing your next words could make or break the deal. Or that moment when you check your phone and discover a scathing public criticism of your work, and shame washes over you like a wave.

We've all experienced the parent-child dynamic that can instantly transport us back to feeling like a powerless child, regardless of our age or accomplishments. And who hasn't felt that sinking feeling after making a significant mistake that impacts others, when self-criticism spirals into a harsh internal dialogue that helps no one?

These moments test our ability to remain deliberate and thoughtful. They challenge us to find that crucial space between stimulus and response, the space where our power lies.

Here are six techniques that have helped me create that crucial space between stimulus and response:

- **Pause and count to ten:** This classic method creates a moment of calm when emotions feel overwhelming. I've found it particularly effective in fast-paced business environments where quick decisions are expected but rarely required.

- **Focus on your breath:** Slow, deliberate breathing anchors you to the present moment. Try breathing in for four counts, holding for two, and exhaling for six. This pattern activates your parasympathetic nervous system, effectively interrupting the stress response.

- **Ground yourself:** Feel the ground beneath your feet, relax your shoulders, and notice five things you can see around you. This technique helps redirect attention away from escalating emotions and back to the physical reality of the moment.

- **Name your emotions:** Simply identifying what you're feeling, "I notice I'm feeling frustrated," can reduce its intensity. This practice creates distance between you and the emotion, reminding you that you are experiencing the emotion, not becoming it.

- **Physical reset:** Sometimes a brief change in physical state can interrupt emotional momentum. Excuse yourself to get a glass of water, stretch, or simply change your posture. I've discreetly used this technique in countless high-stakes negotiations.

- **The "what if" pause:** When triggered, ask yourself: "What if I respond with curiosity instead of defensiveness?" This question opens up possibilities beyond your initial reactive impulse.

Other Techniques of Emotional Mastery

Creating a pause before you react to a stimulus is a great way to begin building the skills of taking charge of your emotions. Here is an overview of some other techniques that I have personally found very helpful.

LOWER YOUR VOICE

Have you ever noticed how you naturally lower your voice when comforting someone who's upset? Or how you instinctively soften your tone when trying to connect with a child or someone who's frightened? We seem to intuitively understand this power of softness in certain contexts. What I've learned is how deliberately extending this approach to challenging conversations, even when I'm feeling frustrated or defensive, can completely shift the dynamic.

That's why I have made it a practice that the more I engage in debates or difficult conversations, the more I force my voice to lower and soften. The older I get, and the more experience I acquire in the resolution of conflict, the more careful I become with my word choice, my tone of voice, and my overall approach.

BE LIKE WATER

The concept of being like water is deeply rooted in Eastern philosophy, particularly in Chinese and Japanese cultures. The notion of flexibility and adaptability is central to Taoism. Lao Tzu, in the *Tao Te Ching,* famously said, "Water is fluid, soft, and yielding. But water will wear away rock, which is rigid and cannot yield. As a rule, whatever is fluid, soft, and yielding will overcome whatever is rigid and hard. This is another paradox: What is soft is strong."

In Japanese culture, the principle of *mizu no kokoro* (mind like water) from Zen Buddhism emphasizes a calm, adaptable state of mind, reflecting water's ability to remain undisturbed and to adapt to its surroundings. This philosophy is often applied in martial arts to maintain mental clarity and composure.

Apply the "Be Like Water" philosophy in conflicts:

Adapt Your Approach: Be flexible and responsive, adjusting your communication style as needed.

Use Softness and Persistence: Approach conflicts with a soft tone and gentle demeanor, while persistently working toward a resolution.

Find Common Ground: Navigate around obstacles by addressing underlying concerns and seeking areas of agreement.

> **Focus on Nonverbal Cues:** Use open body language and a calm tone to reinforce your verbal messages.

> **Stay Calm and Composed:** Emulate the *mizu no kokoro* mindset, maintaining mental clarity and composure.

LEAN INTO EMPATHY

Leaning into empathy means understanding the situation from the other person's perspective. Empathy doesn't necessarily mean agreement, but it shows that we respect and acknowledge the other person's feelings and viewpoints. For me to lean into empathy, it helps if I pause and ask myself: What is that person afraid of right now? What do they need in this very moment? Shifting focus to their emotions and needs often provides clarity and diffuses my own heightened state. This powerful act of redirecting attention allows me to master my emotions and respond with more deliberation.

Form matters, and practicing this form during conflicts and difficult conversations can lead to more harmonious and effective interactions. By being adaptable, soft, and persistent, and by focusing on nonverbal cues, we can navigate even the most challenging conversations with grace and achieve meaningful resolutions.

This isn't just theoretical advice. In my corporate workshops and private sessions, I regularly work with executives who are brilliant strategically but struggle when emotions run high in meetings.

During a session in Montreal, a company's leadership team was fragmenting over budget decisions. Voices were raised, people were interrupting each other, and the CFO had started attending meetings virtually to avoid the tension.

I taught them a simple exercise: "If we were on the same team, we would . . ." When triggered during disagreements, they learned to pause and complete that sentence. "If we were on the same team, we would want to understand why the marketing budget matters so much to you." "If we were on the same team, we would find a way to protect both growth and cash flow."

Within three meetings, their decision-making time had been cut in half because they weren't spending energy managing emotional reactions. The CFO started attending meetings in person again. "I'm not afraid of the tension anymore," she told me. "I can actually focus on the work now instead of managing everyone's reactions."

EMOTIONAL MASTERY IS NOT CAPITULATION

Understanding our emotions is one thing; choosing how to respond to them is another. True emotional mastery manifests in our ability to recognize that if we can control our initial responses to conflict and choose a response that aligns with our deeper values, we can create collaboration.

I am all for standing up for our beliefs, and for protecting those who cannot stand up for themselves. My personal goal when standing up for myself and others is to be effective at it, regardless of how others may see my actions. I want to actually move the needle, to create an opportunity for change. And, based on my personal experience and on my observations of others' conflicts and difficult conversations, we are much more effective when we can speak calmly and listen fully, instead of fighting. If that is what is meant by presenting negativity with positivity, then that is fine with me.

I've learned that being soft doesn't mean being weak. There's remarkable power in gentleness. By lowering our voices, softening our approach, and adapting like water, we create space for real collaboration to happen. This approach isn't about avoiding difficult topics or surrendering our position. It's about choosing a form that makes true communication possible. When we stop trying to overpower others with volume or force, we often discover they become more willing to hear us. It's a simple shift with profound results: speak more softly, and people lean in to listen. Move with flexibility rather than rigidity, and solutions emerge that rigid approaches might never uncover. In conflicts large and small, I've found that the softest voice is often the one that carries furthest.

This simple phrase "you are in charge of you" has been my mantra for a long time, guiding me through countless personal and professional situations. Yet, even after years of practice, I still find myself in the process of learning and growing in this area. Mastering our emotions is one of the hardest tasks we face. It demands patience, discipline, and a commitment to act deliberately, no matter the circumstance.

And yet, I know this: Without mastering my emotions, I cannot build or maintain bridges between myself and other people. Without being in charge of myself, I risk letting my emotions dictate my actions in ways that increase conflict and hinder collaboration, understanding, and trust.

We've all been there. Those moments when emotions took over and we said or did something we later regretted. Whether it's an impulsive word, a hasty decision, or a tone we wish we could take back, these instances remind us just how difficult emotional mastery can be.

Step 3

HAVE A CUP OF TEA

	State	Step 1	Step 2	Step 3
PRINCIPLE 1 Engage with Presence	From Discomfort to Courage	Let's Get Real	You Are In Charge of You	**Have a Cup of Tea**

I met my Chinese business partner, Hong Zhou, literally over a cup of tea. That was one of those moments in life when the tide turned, and I would not be where I am today if not for that cup of tea. I am forever grateful for being there at the right time and right place, and for sitting down to take that cup of tea with him.

We met when I was twenty years old, back in Shanghai, a hopeful, naïve, and highly energetic young foreigner in a sea of locals, looking for a way to start my own business in this modern metropolis. I did not have any business friends or connections, no business or management experience, and no money to invest.

One day, I found myself on the busiest shopping street in downtown Shanghai, Huai Hai Road. It was buzzing with life, crowds of people flowed in and out of stores, their hands full of shopping bags, their chatter lively and animated. Standing on an over-the-street bridge connecting two bustling roads, I felt both exhilarated and overwhelmed. The energy of the place was electric, and I couldn't help but think, "I want to be a part of this!"

So, I decided I would open my own store in Shanghai and sell something wonderful to these thousands of happy shoppers. And how hard can that be?

For the next month, I threw myself into research. Every day, I walked the length of Huai Hai Road, observing shoppers and vendors, scribbling notes in my little notebook about prices, discounts, styles, and customer behaviors. I was that weird foreigner standing in the corner, smiling to herself as she wrote furiously. Most people let me be, and some, out of curiosity, even answered my endless questions:

"How much do you earn per day?"

"How many of these bags did you sell today?"

"What's your most popular item, and why?"

"How much is your store rent? How many employees do you have? How do you market your store?"

They humored me kindly, probably finding my enthusiasm both amusing and harmless. I rewarded them with big, grateful smiles, as if they were handing me gold.

One store, in particular, stood out to me. It was a tiny bag shop with a narrow entrance, squeezed between two larger buildings. It looked unassuming, almost hidden, and yet it was the busiest store on the strip. Every time I visited, it was packed with customers, some buying two or three bags at a time. The energy inside was electric, bags flew off the shelves like hotcakes, and the chatter of the vendors and their excited customers created a constant hum of activity.

For more than a week, I returned to this store every day, spending hours observing the frenzy. I couldn't figure it out. What is going on here? Why is this tiny store so much busier than all the others? Who came up with this concept, and what's the secret to its success?

I had to figure out the secret of their success, so that I could achieve my dream of finally starting a business!

On my last "shift" of observation, a Chinese gentleman approached me. He was in his forties, wearing glasses, with a kind face and a quiet, grounded demeanor. Dressed neatly in business attire, he exuded confidence and calm. Smiling at me, he said: "I've been watching you. You've been here every day for a week, and I hear you've also visited my other stores. Thank you for your interest in my business. I'm Hong Zhou, the owner of this chain of bag stores. Would you like to ask me some questions?"

I was stunned. Did I have questions for him? Absolutely!

"Would you like to go have a cup of tea in the tea house next door?" he asked.

I often think back to that moment. Saying yes to that cup of tea was one of the best decisions of my life. It was, without a doubt, the most educational and auspicious cup of tea I have ever had.

The tea house itself was unassuming yet serene, a quiet oasis tucked away from the chaos of Huai Hai Road. It had simple wooden furniture, the faint aroma of jasmine and oolong teas, and an atmosphere that seemed to encourage deep conversation. Sitting across from Hong Zhou, I felt both excited and nervous. Here was someone who could unlock the mystery I had been trying to solve for weeks.

Over the course of that conversation, Hong Zhou not only answered my questions but also shared insights that would shape my approach to business and life. He explained that the success of his stores came down to a combination of factors: a deep understanding of his market, a strong product-market fit, treating employees like family, sharing profits and cultivating trust, and a pricing strategy that hit the sweet spot for his customers. But beyond the technicalities, there was something more intangible yet equally important.

"You see how our entrance is very narrow?" he asked, his eyes sparkling with humor. "Why do you think that is?"

I didn't have an answer.

"People always go into stores that look crowded," he explained. "They don't want to miss out on something good. Our narrow entrances make the stores look busier, which attracts even more customers. It's simple human psychology."

That tea house conversation marked the beginning of a partnership that would span decades. Hong Zhou and I became business partners, and over the next twenty-eight years, we built numerous ventures together. He taught me about Chinese business culture, helped me grow as a leader, and became one of my closest confidants. His wit, encyclopedic knowledge of Chinese literature, and high emotional intelligence have been invaluable in my personal and professional life.

This cup of tea with Hong Zhou would be the first of many profound lessons China would teach me about conflict and collaboration. In the years that followed, from mah-jongg tables to business negotiations, I would discover how presence leads to curiosity, curiosity enables listening, and listening creates the foundation for meaningful questions, the very pathway of collaboration we're exploring in this book.

That cup of tea with Hong Zhou became a principle I still follow: When we are about to do something challenging, especially emotionally, it is best to slow down to be deliberate with our words and actions. And in honor of Hong Zhou, I refer to this process of slowing down until we can be deliberate with our words and actions as "having a cup of tea."

This phrase doesn't just mean drinking tea. It's about doing something together with the person in front of you that allows both of you to relax your bodies, slow down your breathing, and pay attention to your emotions and state of mind. It's about creating a moment where you can truly notice the human being in front of you, beyond the conflict, beyond the differences. These are the first steps to developing trust.

So let's share a cup of tea in this chapter.

THE SCIENCE OF CONNECTION

There's something almost magical that happens when we share simple moments together: sipping tea, walking side by side, or just sitting in comfortable silence. I've experienced this countless times, that inexplicable sense of connection that emerges even without words.

Science has given us a fascinating window into why these shared moments feel so powerful. Our brains contain what neuroscientists call "mirror neurons" that activate not just when we do something, but when we watch someone else do it too. It's as if my brain rehearses your movements internally when I observe you, creating a subtle bridge between us at the neural level.

I love thinking about this when sharing tea with a new acquaintance. As we both lift our cups, our brains are mirroring each other's actions, creating a silent conversation beneath our spoken one. I've felt this resonance develop during business meetings in China when sharing tea became a ritual of connection before any contracts were signed. What looks like a simple social custom actually creates the neural foundations for trust and understanding even across language barriers and cultural differences.

This isn't just mechanical mimicry; it's how our brains naturally attune to others, allowing us to sense their emotions and intentions. No wonder these shared experiences feel so meaningful; we're literally syncing up at a biological level, creating connection without saying a word.

Best of all, as I've observed, using rituals to create connection makes it more difficult for conflict to take the lead in the dance.

RITUALS FROM AROUND THE WORLD

While sharing a cup of tea is my personal favorite, many cultures have rituals that create similar moments of connection. What rituals do you have in your life or culture that slow you down and bring people together?

- **Drinking maté.** In Argentina, Uruguay, and Paraguay, drinking maté is a cherished tradition. One person prepares this herbal tea in a gourd with a metal straw and passes it around. Everyone drinks from the same gourd, regardless of social status. When you accept a gourd of maté, you're accepting a moment of collaboration.

- **Walking meetings.** Walking alongside someone removes the formality of sitting across a table and creates partnership. I've found walking meetings particularly helpful for sensitive topics. Moving forward together often mirrors the progress you want to make in the conversation.

- **Forest bathing.** In Japan, *shinrin-yoku,* or forest bathing, is a leisurely walk designed to reduce stress and enhance well-being. Living in Northern California for twelve years, I practiced this daily in the redwoods with friends and colleagues. The shared serenity allowed us to let down our defenses and engage in deeper conversations.

- **Sharing food.** Across cultures, sharing a meal creates collaboration. In Ethiopia, *gursha* (feeding someone with your hands) is a gesture of love and respect. In South Korea, communal dishes encourage interaction. Food slows us down and reminds us of our shared humanity.

- **Ping-pong meetings.** I have a customer in Chicago with a ping-pong table in their meeting room. Before every business meeting, they invite visitors to play. I've played several times and watched others after their games. Their flushed cheeks and big smiles make it clear that trust is built through shared joy.

THE POWER OF SPACE AND STILLNESS

A "cup of tea" is not just about the tea. It's about creating deliberate moments of connection through pauses and intentional presence. It's about creating space. Space to ponder the potential differences or conflicts between you and another person, space to slow down, to notice the person across from you. Whether it's tea, maté, or a walk in the woods, these shared rituals remind us that trust and connection begin with presence.

So, what's your "cup of tea"? It could be a quiet walk in the park, a shared meal cooked side by side, folding laundry together while catching up, listening to music with someone you care about, or sitting on a bench or in a café watching the world go by.

Try it today, whatever your version of a "cup of tea" may be, and watch how it transforms your relationships, one small moment at a time.

KEEPING PRESENT DURING CONFLICT

Conflict isn't something to avoid or merely tolerate. It's a pathway to deeper collaboration and growth when approached with presence. When you engage fully in difficult moments, you discover that the discomfort of conflict contains valuable information about what matters most to both parties. The goal isn't to win or change minds, but to learn about yourself, others, and the rich territory where differences meet.

Practice this three-step approach to transformative conflict:

1. Get real by noticing what's actually happening versus the story you're creating. Ask yourself "What are the facts here?" instead of assuming intentions or meanings. For example, recognize "They disagree with my idea" rather than jumping to "They think I'm incompetent."

2. Master your emotions by pausing to breathe and creating space between stimulus and response. Intentionally soften your voice, relax your shoulders, and slow your pace, remembering

that softness often proves more powerful than force in difficult conversations.

3. Create a "cup of tea" moment where you slow down enough to be truly present with each other. This might be literal (sharing a beverage) or figurative (taking a walk together), but the key is establishing a shared space where collaboration can happen before diving into disagreement.

Start small. This week, identify one uncomfortable conversation you've been avoiding.

- Before engaging, write down what you hope to learn rather than what you hope to achieve.

- During the conversation, ask questions that reveal values rather than just positions: "What matters most to you about this?"

- After the conversation, reflect: What surprised you about their perspective? What did you discover about your own values?

Notice how approaching conflict with curiosity rather than certainty transforms these moments from battlegrounds into open conversations where genuine collaboration becomes possible.

Reassurance: Start Where You Are

You don't need to become a different person to practice these principles. You don't need to suddenly become bold or outspoken. Start with tiny conflicts: the moment when you want extra sauce but don't want to bother the server, the meeting where you have a different opinion but usually stay quiet, the family dinner where you typically change the subject when things get tense.

Loving conflict begins with loving yourself enough to speak up for what matters to you, even in small ways.

Principle 2

ASSUME NOTHING

*	State	Step 1	Step 2	Step 3
PRINCIPLE 2 **Assume** **Nothing**	From Close-Minded to Curious	There Is Enough	Notice It, Name It, Express It	We Are All Doing Our Best

From Close-Minded to Curious

Have you ever caught yourself filling in the blanks of someone else's story? I've shared several examples in this book of how my mind rushes to fill in blanks with assumptions. Here's yet another example from my own experience:

> I met Nicolas through our shared love of sourdough bread
> that I had acquired while living in San Francisco. As soon
> as I moved to France, I looked for bakeries that made
> the sourdough bread I so loved. Nicolas had just started

exploring baking his own bread in Saint Denis, a northern suburb of Paris.

As soon as I heard that he wanted to bake his own bread, the entrepreneur in me immediately jumped to conclusions: He wants to bake lots of bread, create his own brand, sell it all over Paris, and become the most successful sourdough bread maker in the city. I was already imagining his growth path and success story.

It was like a cold shower for me to watch Nicolas's actual process. He does indeed bake his own bread (including the best sourdough I've ever had) *but* without any of the other aspects I had assumed. He works just once a week, waking up early at four a.m. and working till four p.m. He makes just enough bread to sell to one co-op in Saint Denis and to bring in just enough revenue to pay his rent, buy food, and cover expenses for the oven.

No brand. No growth. No extra shifts. No employees so that he can scale up. Nothing that I would do or that many of my entrepreneur friends would recognize as success. *And* he has a great lifestyle, spending all the other days of the week resting, reading, writing, volunteering, walking, and simply living.

Now and then I still ask him the usual questions entrepreneurs ask themselves: What is your vision for the future of your activity? What is your goal? What is your exit strategy? He smiles and shrugs. He is good where he is.

What's important for him is that he is fully aligned with his values: no extra pollution on the planet, no extra footprint from his activities on the community, maintaining collaboration with his neighbors, and being good to himself.

I've learned so much from Nicolas and our conversations. I've gained appreciation for our differences and come to understand that we can both be right. Both lifestyles are possible and valid. I've seen how important it is to be first and foremost aligned with your values before striving for more, and that more is not always better.

Our minds are meaning-making machines, constantly filling gaps in our knowledge with stories we create based on our assumptions about the person or our prejudices. When someone doesn't respond to our message, they must be ignoring us. When a colleague disagrees with our idea, they must not respect us. When someone from a different political background speaks, we assume we already know what they'll say.

These assumptions, often unconscious, nearly always unexamined, are usually more likely to feed the fire of conflict and erect barriers to genuine collaboration. They close our minds before there's even a chance for curiosity to flourish. They replace the messy, beautiful complexity of human experience with flat caricatures that rarely reflect reality.

Assuming nothing is about recognizing the stories we tell ourselves and holding those stories at a distance. It's about approaching each person, each situation, with fresh eyes. Not erasing our experience but remaining open to what might surprise us.

I've learned this lesson through countless humbling moments: in boardrooms where I misjudged a quiet colleague, in relationships where I filled silences with feared meanings, and when Nicolas the baker challenged my assumptions about success. Each time I catch myself assuming, I try to pause and wonder, "What don't I know here?"

While the presence we cultivated in the previous section creates the attentional space for collaboration, this second principle, Assume Nothing, fills that space with curiosity rather than judgment. The ability to engage with presence gives us the foundation to then question our assumptions and approach others with genuine openness.

CROSS-CULTURAL ASSUMPTIONS

In the spring of 1994, I was invited to a traditional wedding in Chengdu, the capital of Sichuan Province in southwest China. It was my first Chinese wedding experience, and I did not know what to expect. Entering a large courtyard, I saw the sea of Chinese guests all looking at me with surprise and curiosity at the only foreigner at this gathering.

"*Laowai! Laowai!*" I heard many of them say aloud, with kids pointing their little fingers at me and laughing. *Laowai* means *old foreigner.* No matter how often my Chinese friends assured me this is not an insult, I still felt excluded, clearly identified as not one of the community. It made me feel sad and frustrated, since I spent all my time and energy learning about the language and culture, trying to belong. Yet no matter how much I tried, how well I spoke the language and understood the culture, I looked different, and as such, I was a *laowai.*

Happily, I did not have to stew in this feeling of being alienated for too long. I was not the main attraction I would soon find out! The first (and as I understood later) and only main activity at this celebration was mah-jongg. This was going to be a pop quiz of my knowledge of Chinese culture and my ability to belong.

The guests came into the courtyard and were immediately seated at square tables positioned all around the place in groups of four. The tiles were mixed, and the sound of falling tiles and excited chatting filled the air. The beautiful bride and groom went around the tables to greet guests and witness their skillful playing. Laughter, cigarette smoke, and falling tiles were the music of this wedding, and I wanted to be included.

I asked to play and was met by shocked stares. "*Laowai* playing mah-jongg?"

Yet I was given a chair at a table with three old men, their fingers yellow from tobacco, who were chain-smoking and openly laughing at their new companion. My boyfriend stood next to my chair, sheepishly trying to make excuses for the cigarette smoke I was forced to inhale and for the clear mistrust and mocking by my partners.

Everything changed once we started playing and I won the first game! Mocking stopped, and instead I caught some serious surprised stares from my companions. They started making conversation with me, asking me where I was from, who taught me how to play, and why I was so fluent in Chinese.

I was so focused on winning; I did not look up. The next time I did, though, the bride and groom were standing next to us and the table was surrounded by guests watching us play and chat.

"*Laowai* can play mah-jongg!"

A line of new players formed next to our table as guests tried to sit at our table to play with me. I was not that good at mah-jongg, so this was not at all like the chess players competing to play with the grand master. I think it was mostly the curiosity of experiencing an integral part of their own culture with someone different from them who clearly loved and respected it, and wanted to learn.

Over several hours, I got to meet most of the wedding party this way. I received so much knowledge and so many stories and tips about Chinese culture at that mah-jongg table. From actual playing tips to places to eat, books to read, mountains to climb, people to meet. But mostly, I received their welcome and their trust: welcome to their community, their way of being, and their hearts; trust with their wisdom, collaborations, and friendships.

Looking back on that wedding day, I realize something fundamental about human connection: When we make the effort to participate in what matters to others, which could be their games, their traditions, their celebrations, we create opportunities for genuine belonging. My ability to play mah-jongg wasn't extraordinary, but my willingness to engage fully in this cultural touchstone made all the difference. The initial label of "outsider" fell away as shared experience took center stage.

> *"True belonging doesn't require you to change who you are;*
> *it requires you to be who you are."*
>
> **—BRENÉ BROWN**

As my mah-jongg experience showed, sometimes life offers us unexpected opportunities to challenge our assumptions so we can build connections and relationships.

NOTHING IN COMMON? THINK AGAIN.

One of the most insidious assumptions we make about other people who are different from us is that we have nothing in common with them. But in my work, I've found that is never true. I moderate groups who have strong disagreements. Over the years, I've noticed a common thread: *While assumptions divide us, shared fears connect us.* When participants realize they share the same fears, they feel an immediate bond, and the collaboration that follows from the bond builds trust and respect. People are able to overcome whatever prejudices and assumptions they had when coming into the meeting.

I saw this clearly in one of the Hope sessions I mentioned in Chapter 1 where the pro-Palestinian and pro-Israel participants met virtually to share, connect, and learn from each other. Our compassionate moderator was Jesús de la Garza, CEO and founder of Monarch Leaders. With over thirty years of experience in business and counseling, he specializes in moderating high-stakes group interactions and resolving conflicts, making him an expert in transformative leadership and team dynamics. I am honored to call Jesús my coach and mentor.

During one meeting, Jesús asked us to share the biggest fears that the Gaza conflict stirred in us. We all spoke, one after another.

And we were all shocked to discover that despite all our differences, that we stood on the other side of the fence of this horrible conflict, and that most of us came from different countries and cultures, we all had very similar fears:

- Fears for our families' well-being

- Fears of not belonging fully to our group

- Fears of governmental control, if there was mistrust of our governments or the people in power

- Fears of becoming too angry and, as such, being insensitive to other people's pain and suffering

- Fears of being misunderstood, dismissed, disrespected, or labeled

When the last person finished, we all sensed the change in the virtual room. We saw each other more clearly. We respected and trusted each other. We actually felt love and care for everyone there.

As a result of that meeting, I now have a new tool when I moderate such groups or am a part of a difficult discussion. When I see that respect, trust, or connection is missing, or that people are not truly listening to each other, or getting defensive or self-righteous, I often resort to this one simple, yet extremely powerful, tool that Jesús taught me. I ask all the participants to take turns and share. I either go first or ask someone in the room to start as long as I know this person usually shares deeply and vulnerably. That depth of sharing sets the stage for others to do the same.

"What is your biggest fear about this subject?" I ask.

Merely asking this question changes the atmosphere in the room, and we can see and feel it even in a virtual environment. Faces literally change from lacking focus to sharp focus.

And every time, it works wonders.

Opening up about our fears opens the path to vulnerability and honesty. From there, connection and respect are the natural results.

CHECKING ASSUMPTIONS ABOUT YOURSELF

My second immigration after going to China from my family home was to the United States.

The first time I saw the tall, majestic redwood trees of the Bay Area of Northern California, I felt like I was at home there. Walking into the forest of these gigantic, powerful trees felt like walking into a sacred temple. I was in deep awe and filled with admiration as I experienced the transcendence that nature gives us. I wanted to be there every day and to never leave, so that I could keep experiencing the sweet feeling of humility in front of the majesty and beauty of nature.

Every chance I got, sometimes daily, I went to hike the trails among the redwood trees. I often wondered about the intense and powerful feeling of comfort that the redwoods provoked in me. I think it was due to a sense of certainty I felt. Certainty that they had and would always be there, notwithstanding the weather, pollution, or human activities.

It took me months to realize what was really happening: I was seeking certainty in nature because I'd discovered how uncertain I actually was about most things in my life. In this way, the redwoods became my teachers in a different way than I expected. I had assumed I was someone who embraced uncertainty. After all, I'd left everything familiar to live in different countries. But the redwoods showed me I was actually carrying a hidden need for certainty somewhere, somehow. This realization changed how I approached difficult conversations.

It also served as a reminder that while I'm trying to consciously fight the assumptions I make about other people, I need to be careful not to do the same thing to myself. Understanding myself better leads to a stronger connection with myself, which gives me a calmness I can use to create collaboration with others.

And now I challenge you to do the same for yourself. What assumptions are you making about your motivations, fears, desires? How can you be certain of those motivations? How are your assumptions shaping your actions for better or worse?

THE FREEDOM OF ASSUMING NOTHING

In tango, there is a moment when two dancers first meet on the floor, a moment of pure potential. The *lead* extends an invitation, and the *follow* accepts, but what happens next depends entirely on their willingness to set aside assumptions and be present with each other. If either dancer arrives with rigid expectations, about the music, the steps, or their partner's abilities, the dance becomes mechanical, constrained. But when both approach with openness, something magical unfolds: a dance unique to that moment, that pair, that music.

I've found that there are three steps that help us become more open-minded:

	State	Step 1	Step 2	Step 3
PRINCIPLE 2 Assume Nothing	From Close-Minded to Curious	There Is Enough	Notice It, Name It, Express It	We Are All Doing Our Best

- **Step 1: There is enough.** Learn to acknowledge to ourselves that there is enough, enough time, recognition, and success, for all of us, which frees us from the scarcity mindset that fuels many assumptions.

- **Step 2: Notice it, name it, express it.** Notice, name, and express your assumptions, bringing them into the light where they have less power.

- **Step 3: We are all doing our best.** Embrace the mindset that we are all doing our best with what we have, which grants us compassion for ourselves and others.

These three elements of assuming nothing: embracing abundance, recognizing our assumptions, and extending compassion because we are all doing our best, work together as an integrated practice to help us move beyond assumptions and build collaborations. When we assume nothing, we create space for everything: for deeper understanding that supersedes conflict, for genuine surprise, for collaboration that transcends our preconceptions. In my experience, when used together, these principles emphasize abundance thinking, which creates space for multiple perspectives; naming our assumptions gives us power to question them; and compassion allows us to connect despite our differences.

The steps may feel challenging at first. I still struggle with them sometimes, finding myself crafting elaborate stories about others' intentions or falling into judgment before I've gathered the facts. We're all simply practicing, learning to approach each other with more curiosity and less certainty.

What I've discovered is this: We open ourselves to the possibility that reality might be richer, more complex, and more hopeful than our assumptions could ever predict.

What I find so liberating about the practice of assuming nothing is that it doesn't ask us to know everything; it simply invites us to acknowledge how little we truly know with certainty. There's freedom in this admission, a lightness that comes from releasing the burden of having to be right about others before we've truly listened.

The practice of assuming nothing creates the fertile ground in which true listening can take root. And it is through listening, deep, curious, compassionate listening, that we begin to see beyond conflict to find connection and collaboration.

Step 1

THERE IS ENOUGH

	State	Step 1	Step 2	Step 3
PRINCIPLE 2 Assume Nothing	From Close- Minded to Curious	**There Is Enough**	Notice It, Name It, Express It	We Are All Doing Our Best

The fear of scarcity, of not getting enough, versus the feeling that there is enough is what many of us experience in our daily lives in different settings. We often fear that there isn't enough time, love, attention, or that there isn't enough recognition, success, or wins. There may not seem to be enough money to meet our needs, enough opportunities to fulfill our potential, or enough support to overcome challenges. This sense of scarcity can permeate our relationships, our work, and even our sense of self-worth.

And while there is surely an objective reality to many of us not having equal access to information, resources, and power, in this chapter we specifically look at our *own perception of reality* and how this perception of either having enough or not enough influences our ability to connect with others.

I've noted that that mindset of scarcity ("I do not have enough") often leads to competition and mistrust, holding us back from true connection. The fear of scarcity of time, resources, or recognition is a very uncomfortable state of mind that places limits on us and our relationships with others. We may worry that someone else's influence means a loss of our own, or that another person's skills will overshadow ours. This fear drives us to protect what we have, often at the cost of relationships, collaboration, and innovation. We see others not as potential partners but as threats, making it difficult to build true collaborations or find collective success.

Having a scarcity mindset also leads us to close our mind and see fewer options and opportunities. We end up thinking, "It's us versus them. Either we win or we lose." It's nearly impossible to stay curious or open-minded while thinking these kind of thoughts. Getting stuck within this framework can also lead to seeing other people as a potential enemy.

In his book *Long Walk to Freedom*, Nelson Mandela showed how deeply he understood the destructive power of division when he famously said, "When we dehumanize and demonize our opponents, we abandon the possibility of peacefully resolving our differences, and seek to justify violence against them." This insight perfectly captures how a scarcity mindset can escalate from simple competition to dangerous dehumanization, making genuine collaboration impossible.

Let's research how changing our mindset from scarcity to abundance plays out in different settings.

AT HOME: DEVELOPING THIS MINDSET WITH YOUR CHILDREN

While we can find the scarcity mindset in multiple settings in our daily personal and working lives, it's particularly evident with children, where we see the dynamics of perceived scarcity play out frequently.

In my house, these exchanges between my three children might go something like this:

> "Why did she get to play on her iPad five minutes longer than me?"

> "It's not fair that he got more cookies than me!"

> "You took her out on a fun activity three times this month, and me only twice!"

And no matter how long and how patiently we explain that everyone gets to have the iPad the same amount of time, that there are more cookies coming out of the oven, or that the next activity with them is already planned for next week, it doesn't seem to help.

So, we began teaching our kids the mindset we call "there is enough." We started noticing a shift as soon as we encouraged the children to make decisions for themselves, such as how many cookies each would get, or even bake the cookies themselves. They understood they could always just bake more! The same happened with iPad time, which we strictly limit. As soon as it became up to them to ensure they all got the same amount of time, they became more willing to compromise for each other.

And now that they each decide where we go for separate activities, they are in full control of their experiences with us, focusing more on choosing well instead of paying all their attention to what their siblings get.

Recently, for example, when my family was deciding on weekend activities, my oldest suggested that instead of comparing who got to do what, each child should create a wish list of experiences they wanted to have in the coming months. This shifted their focus from comparing their activities to imagining and planning experiences they genuinely desired.

Beyond sharing resources, we also focus significant time on practicing gratitude and generosity. We share what we're grateful for during family meals, creating a ritual of appreciation rather than comparison. We make joint decisions about charities and projects we donate to or serve at, involving the children in these decisions. This contributes to creating a family culture of "there is enough" by showing them that we have not just enough for ourselves, but enough to share with others.

When children believe there is enough to go around, they instinctively relax and open their minds to curiosity, to a world of possibilities, and to unique, creative solutions. This leads to more team spirit and cooperation. We also teach them that natural resources are not limitless, and we need to use them with care, ensuring sustainability for future generations.

What I've learned over the years is the shift to "there is enough" thinking isn't just important for children; it's essential for all of us.

SCARCITY VS. ABUNDANCE IN BUSINESS

I've watched scarcity thinking play out in companies for years. People withhold information because they're afraid someone else might look better. Leaders micromanage because they worry about getting credit. Fear of limited resources kills creativity and turns potential collaborators into competitors.

When I started my businesses, I noticed something about myself. When I gripped tightly to what I had, afraid there wouldn't be enough elsewhere, my work started feeling like a prison. I'd catch myself thinking, "I'd better hold on to this client because who knows if I'll find another one," or, "I can't take this risk because what if I fail?"

These thoughts felt protective. But they kept me stuck.

When I shifted to "there is enough," things changed. I could share ideas freely. I could mentor others without fearing they'd surpass me. I could walk away from clients or projects that weren't working anymore. Not because I was being reckless, but because I trusted my skills had value and there would be other opportunities.

I've watched this same shift in others. Someone stops holding their breath every time a contract comes up for renewal. They start collaborating instead of competing. They take risks they couldn't before.

On to the Bigger World

An abundance mindset doesn't just apply to resources or recognition. It extends to how we view people who hold fundamentally different worldviews from our own. When we believe there's enough room for different perspectives, we can approach those differences with curiosity rather than defense.

Jonathan Haidt talks about expanding our circle of "common humanity," focusing on what connects us rather than what divides us. Martin Luther King Jr. and Nelson Mandela both used this approach, calling on people to recognize their shared humanity rather than fostering an "us versus them" mentality.

Some people argue this oversimplifies complex issues or minimizes the unique struggles of marginalized groups. They're right that we can't ignore systemic injustices. But in my experience recognizing our shared humanity while also addressing specific grievances isn't either-or. It's both-and. We can build empathy and justice at the same time.

WHAT AN ABUNDANCE MINDSET LOOKS LIKE IN PRACTICE

Here's what I've seen work when trying to shift toward abundance thinking:

Focus on what you have, not what you lack. When our design team faced budget cuts, we created a "resource inventory" of everything we already had, from unused software licenses to overlooked talent. We found opportunities we hadn't considered.

Look for solutions where everyone benefits. A client and I recently turned a pricing disagreement into a phased plan that protected their budget while securing our revenue goals. During negotiations, I aim for agreements that allow all parties to benefit. This builds lasting partnerships not just transactional relationships.

Notice when leaders acknowledge that good ideas come from anywhere. I've seen teams transform when leadership stops hoarding credit and starts supporting growth. These small shifts create space for real collaboration through conflict, not despite it. I watched this happen at a global company facing severe budget constraints. Instead of cutting training and innovation, leadership launched cross-department projects, encouraged low-cost innovation ideas, and created peer-mentoring programs. People stopped protecting what they had and started building together.

This is why I do this work. I've seen what scarcity thinking does between colleagues, between families, between countries vying for resources. Every negotiation becomes a battle to be won. But when we shift to "there is enough," something else becomes possible. Creative diplomacy. Solutions where everyone gets what they need. Even with finite resources, collaboration can unlock what competition never could.

Step 2

NOTICE IT, NAME IT, EXPRESS IT

	State	Step 1	Step 2	Step 3
PRINCIPLE 2 Assume Nothing	From Close-Minded to Curious	There Is Enough	**Notice It, Name It, Express It**	We Are All Doing Our Best

We are often not aware of all the judgments we carry. Discovering my own judgments has become a committed practice for me. In fact, I see undiscovered judgments and biases as my blind spots. And just as I would rather not drive with large blind spots on busy roads, I do everything possible to uncover my judgments and biases about other people when I interact with them.

Before we interact with other people, we need to check in with ourselves about what preconceived ideas we may carry and what judgments may arise in us. We cannot do away with or delay preconceived judgments unless we are aware we have them. That is why this process is extremely important.

For example, while growing up in a Soviet and post-Soviet society, we were taught to judge a person's worth solely by what was outwardly visible. Everyone focused on how we dressed and what cars we drove. I saw the same bias in Chinese society, so that behavior was even more deeply ingrained in me after living there. As a result, when I started my life in the United States, I continued to judge people by how they dressed and other material possessions. But as I spent more time and increasingly exposed myself to others in the US, I began to *notice* how little my American acquaintances cared about what others or they wore or what cars they or others drove. Maybe even more important, I *noticed* that they didn't judge me by outward signs and symbols. That was when I started to slowly unpack my own biases and perceive the judging behavior that society had ingrained in me. At that point, I was able to start appreciating people for what they say and do and not how they dress.

So how do we uncover faulty judgments or preconceived notions?

We first have to *take notice* or become aware of these thoughts and ideas. This is the first step, where we become conscious of our thoughts, feelings, or sensations without necessarily categorizing them. It is about recognizing something is happening.

Next, we have to *name* these thoughts for ourselves (this could be in writing, or just admitting them to ourselves). This is a step further, identifying and labeling our experience clearly. Naming helps us to confront the thought or feeling with more clarity, making it easier to process and address.

And then we have to *express* our feelings about them (this could be to our close friends, our therapist, or even sometimes to other people).

What's important is to give other people a chance; wait and see what is *actually* happening versus what I *assume* is happening. By doing this, we give ourselves a chance to notice and free ourselves from the inherited ideas and biases so we can judge the situation as it truly is.

A BLIND SPOT UNCOVERED

A preconceived judgment (or blind spot) I grew up with has to do with the realm of relationships. I was taught that men need to feel powerful in their relationships with women. Therefore, girls and women were instructed to let men think that any good idea was automatically theirs and that women should keep our voices and our power hidden. I only discovered this hidden bias in myself when I created a profile on a dating app in my thirties. I felt the need to spell out that only highly successful and ambitious men should apply.

When I was questioned why this was so important to me, I said: "If he has his own strong ambitions, he will let me be me and thrive however I want to. I don't have to pretend to be small and powerless with him."

I now know that a person doesn't need to be ambitious themselves to allow and nurture freedom, ambition, and success in their partners. But I was only able to discover this once I *noticed, named,* and *clearly expressed* false ideas I had inherited about how men are and how women need to treat them.

This was a major blind spot for me that I am still struggling with today. I am more aware of it and speak about it openly since I found that by being open about my judgments and biases I can diminish their power over me.

You may be thinking, "What if I am right?"

If all my assumptions turn out to be true, I can be deliberate about how I'm going to handle those particular situations.

But what does not work is acting based on the wrong assumptions. If I start behaving based on these wrong assumptions without checking their veracity, the situation will very well likely turn into what I am expecting it to be, even if it was not going to do so in the first place.

Challenging Cultural Assumptions

Another assumption I had to confront came from my cultural background about how generations should live together. Growing up in Ukraine, I watched my parents care for their mothers with patience and love. Every weekend brought large gatherings with extended family. Singing, dancing, poetry, and laughter. It truly "took a village" to raise children and care for elders.

When I moved to the United States, I couldn't believe how different things were. During visits to my first husband's grandparents in Florida retirement communities, I witnessed something that challenged all my assumptions about family and care.

What surprised me was how rarely younger people visited, and how social activities were organized to ensure residents didn't stay alone. This was nothing like what I grew up with in Ukraine. Elderly people living separately from family, in structured communities rather than woven into daily family life.

I spent hours talking with residents who had amazing stories to share and wisdom to teach, but few people to listen. I found myself wanting to be everyone's grandchild there, to take in all they desperately wanted to give.

Neither approach is right or wrong. The close-knit interdependence of Ukrainian communities and the organized independence of American retirement communities are different solutions to the same human needs. By noticing my judgmental thoughts ("This is wrong, families should live together") and naming them as cultural assumptions, I could express genuine curiosity instead.

"Tell me how this works for you" became more valuable than "This isn't how we do it."

Assumptions about "the right way" to live can blind us to understanding different approaches. When we notice our judgments, name them as cultural perspectives rather than universal truths, and express genuine curiosity, we can learn from ways of life that initially seem wrong to us.

DEVELOPING YOUR ABILITY TO NAME AND EXPRESS FEELINGS AND IDEAS

Here are five practical tools for developing your assumption awareness:

- **Develop body awareness.** Your body often signals assumption making before your mind does. Notice physical reactions like tension in your shoulders, heat in your face, or tightness in your chest. These are early warning signs that you're creating a narrative about someone's intentions.

- **Complete this sentence: "I notice I'm assuming that ________."** This framework helps you identify the specific story you're creating. For example: "I notice I'm assuming when that person didn't respond to my text, that they were angry with me."

- **Fact vs. story separation.** Write down what you actually observed versus what you're interpreting. Fact: "They didn't make eye contact during the meeting." Story: "They don't respect my ideas." This distinction is crucial for clear thinking.

- **Question your certainty.** When you find yourself thinking, "Obviously they . . ." or, "They clearly . . ." stop and recognize these as assumption signals. It's extremely rare that we can truly be certain about another person's motivations.

- **Test assumptions gently.** Express your interpretation as a hypothesis to be tested, not a fact to be defended. "I'm curious about something. When you didn't respond to my email, I started wondering if you were upset with me. Is that accurate?"

Here are some examples of how I handled preconceived notions or judgments in my daily life by going through the process of noticing, naming, and expressing them.

- Expressed to my mother when I traveled and I left my children with her: "Mom, I am feeling anxious because I think you might be judging me for leaving my kids behind while I travel." I noticed the tension in my body, I named it "feeling anxious," and I expressed it to my mom.

- Expressed to my husband at a fancy French restaurant: "I cannot seem to relax and enjoy the atmosphere and amazing food here, because I assume the waiters are going to be rude and dismissive toward me because I speak French with an accent and do not know the rules and habits of the locals well." I noticed the discomfort and hesitation, I named it "anticipation of rejection," and I expressed it to my husband.

- Expressed to my Chinese colleague before a major negotiation with our Chinese business partners: "I am having trouble concentrating on the actual conversation because I have an assumption that they do not take us seriously or think we are trying to undermine the project." I noticed the lack of concentration, I named it "distrust," and I expressed it to my Chinese colleague.

As you probably noticed, these assumptions *could* all be correct. And they could all be wrong.

IS THIS WHO I WANT TO BE?

To help me in this process of learning to notice, name, and express what I'm experiencing, I love this daily question I learned from the Stoics: Is this who I want to be?

When I realize I am judging people and that my judgment and assumptions stand in the way of us connecting, I ask myself that question. It helps me stop and think. It then centers me in my truth and helps me be more curious, open-minded, and compassionate.

And do you know what happened the first time I went through the practice of notice it, name it, express it? When I expressed my anxiety to my mother about leaving the kids, she reassured me she was proud of my work. When I named my assumptions before the negotiation with my Chinese colleague, we strategized together and the meeting went smoothly. And when I went out to that fancy French restaurant with my husband? The waiter was professional, polite, helpful, and warm toward me and others, and we all had a great time. And now that I have uncovered my faulty judgment about French waiters, I am quickly becoming best friends with every waiter I meet in France!

Step 3

WE ARE ALL DOING OUR BEST

	State	Step 1	Step 2	Step 3
PRINCIPLE 2 Assume Nothing	From Close-Minded to Curious	There Is Enough	Notice It, Name It, Express It	We Are All Doing Our Best

When I met Mr. Zhou, the head of the Chinese manufacturing company we worked with, he looked nothing like a leader I was accustomed to. He was a son of a poor farmer from the poorest areas in China. He had no money to invest in the project we were managing and no employees. Yet he was eager, hungry, committed, and persistent.

One moment in 2006 stands out in my memory: Mr. Zhou picked me and my team up from the train station in his old, beat-up minivan. It was exhaustingly hot, humid, and sticky outside, and we were all tired from the trip and anxious to get on with our day full of factory visits.

However, the van would not start for what felt like an hour. Sweaty Mr. Zhou did everything possible to get us moving and apologized profusely to us for the heat and the wait.

Finally, the broken-down van started, and we all cheered in excitement that we would finally get some air conditioning. But that was not to be. Mr. Zhou explained that the car could not have air conditioning and drive at the same time.

So, there we were, bumping along in a sweltering van for forty-five minutes on our way to his factory, all the while listening to Mr. Zhou's big plans of becoming a super packaging star in China. Our faces were red, and our patience was waning.

At that point, everyone on my team turned against working with Mr. Zhou.

"Anna, he is not the 'type' of partner we are looking for. He has no established customer base, no references. Heck, he doesn't even have air conditioning in his car!"

Yet I felt his hunger, and I asked everyone to drop their judgments and try working with him. "Let's look past what he doesn't have and see what he does have. I couldn't care less about the state of his car, but I love the values that he wants to build this company on. His passion will drive this business forward and we will all win."

In the end, we granted the project to him, and as such, financed his first steps in business. Mr. Zhou now runs Star Packaging, a multibillion-dollar business with one thousand employees and eight major factories around China. He is the leader of the packaging industry in China, with sales offices in the US, Singapore, and Australia. He sells to thirty-five countries with products and inventions with eighty-nine patents. His personal worth is around four to five billion USD. And, as he promised, they are going public next year. He also now drives a lovely car with air conditioning!

From this experience with Mr. Zhou, I learned one simple truth that always works as a cognitive turnaround for me to change or postpone judgments:

> Everyone does the best they can in any given moment
> with the resources they have available to them.

When I say this to myself before interacting with other people, this new mindset softens my judgments. Another way to turn judgments around is to actually question ourselves. Another quote, this time by Viktor Frankl, describes best what I mean: "No man should judge unless he asks himself in absolute honesty whether, in a similar situation, he might not have done the same."

It is striking to realize that Viktor Frankl could still believe this after witnessing horrible atrocities inflicted on human beings by human beings during three years in four Nazi concentration camps. Despite all the pain and fear he undoubtedly experienced, he was able to ask this question of himself.

And one other helpful thought comes from the Dalai Lama:

> *"People take different roads seeking fulfillment and*
> *happiness. Just because they're not on your road doesn't*
> *mean they've gotten lost."*

I am especially grateful for this reminder from the Dalai Lama about our differences and each person's uniqueness. Reminding myself that it is not about right or wrong but instead about the variety of ways in which all humans live and believe, frees me from judging other people's ways.

The recognition that we are all doing our best becomes especially powerful when we encounter people who seem to live in entirely different realities from our own. Whether through politics, culture, or life experience, these differences can feel insurmountable unless and until we approach them with genuine curiosity and compassion, as I've seen in Hope.

DOING OUR BEST DESPITE DIFFERENT REALITIES

As I mentioned, Hope taught me about living in different realities while staying connected. Step by step, we discovered proof of these realities:

- Different news sources reporting conflicting information

- Contrasting images and videos shared on social media

- Varying analyses and interpretations of events

- Divergent historical perspectives

For example, during the US college protests against the war in Gaza in May 2024, we learned that media in the pro-Palestinian camp reported no signs of anti-Semitism and highlighted positive signs of global support for Palestinians. In contrast, pro-Israel media focused heavily on anti-Semitic incidents during these protests, emphasizing Jewish students' negative experiences and concerns. Each group was exposed to vastly different realities, reinforcing existing beliefs and perceptions.

Yet despite our monthly connections and undeniable signs that each of us was living in our own bubbles, many of us found it hard to remember those connections during the following month once we were back in our lives. We preferred to return to our groups and rest in the bubble of information that confirmed our point of view.

Why is that? What happens to us that makes it so hard to apply intellectual humility when we're faced with information that confronts our beliefs?

*What happens to us that makes it so hard to apply
intellectual humility when we are faced with information
that confronts our beliefs?*

What happened in Hope taught me something about all of us. While we created moments of genuine connection and collaboration during our meetings, we still struggled to maintain that perspective once we returned to our separate information worlds. This pattern isn't unique to our group or this particular conflict; it's deeply rooted in how human minds work.

STORIES OF DOING OUR BEST

Can we stay in love and maintain connection with people even when we strongly disagree with them on fundamental values? Can we use conflict to actually enhance these relationships? If so, how?

I have been researching this topic for years now, because I find myself in these kind of situations all the time, involving everything from child rearing and other lifestyle choices to disagreements about capitalism vs. individualistic economies.

For many of us, the Covid pandemic, which raised questions about vaccines and the consequent limitations and lockdowns, brought into relief the major divisions of opinions and beliefs within families, intimate relationships, and business partnerships, among others. And the divisions were extremely potent. For people who had health and safety uppermost in their minds, it was all about survival: the survival of themselves and their loved ones. For people who did not accept limitations directed by the authorities, it was about their personal freedom, which they saw as just as vital as life and death was for the first group. Many relationships did not survive these divisions.

The same starkness of division in values can be seen in the United States between the Democratic and Republican values. Or around the conflict in the Middle East, with people supporting either Israel or the Palestinians. Or in France, the division between political parties on the left and right spectrum. This list goes on and on.

So, what should we be considering when major divisions strike families and close relationships? Is it possible to stay strong in these relationships, and if so, how?

I've asked this question of many people across different countries, lifestyles, and political affiliations. Here are two stories, with identifying details removed. What I've found is that opposition in values feels remarkably similar everywhere. It's a deeply human experience.

Story #1: Business Partners Agree to Disagree

"My business partner and I are opposites when it comes to social backgrounds, lifestyle, and especially, politics. In fact, we have little in common when it comes to how we see and appreciate life. Yet we have been running thriving businesses together for twenty-five years now, and I would not want anyone else as a business partner. I think what allows us to be connected is that business comes first for both of us. We enjoy working together and we do it well. Also, both of us have calm, measured personalities. So, when we discuss matters other than business and we start strongly disagreeing with each other, we do it with serenity, measurement, and respect. So, we never end up truly offending each other. We both share the value of measured, calm debate, choosing our words carefully, checking our facts and sources of information, and listening well. We do debate often, and we strongly disagree with each other as a result. But at the end, business is business. And that is what matters for both of us."

It's clear from Story #1 that shared values and priorities, in this case, putting the business first, can serve as a unifying force even when there are other fundamental disagreements.

Story #2: Managing Well in a Marriage

"My wife and I come from the same cultural background, social strata, and have similar histories in terms of our families, religion, and general life values. We parent our three children well and are in general very strong partners in family and in life. But we do have major disagreements as far as the politics of our country is concerned. Opposite sides of the fence. She on the far left of the spectrum, and I am more on the right. Both of us feel strongly about our point of view, and due to our passionate and strong personalities, our arguments can get extremely loud and heated. We do sometimes say things to each other during these conflicts that we later regret and wish we could walk back on. It is often embarrassing how high the volume of our conflicts can get.

"What we do agree on is that our children should not witness these heated conflicts until we get better at them. Frankly, we are embarrassed we have not found the way to debate in a more measured and calm way, and don't want our children to witness that. So, we only discuss politics when in private since we know our children can probably sense the disagreement now that they are becoming teenagers and more aware of the world around them and the political situation in our country. I am worried about how we will manage our disagreement and such opposite points of view. For now, we agreed that we will each speak to the kids about our point of view, and keep the arguments away from them. Right or wrong, this is where we stand for now. This story is yet to be written."

Story #2 highlights the challenges of managing disagreements when they are passionate and emotionally charged, particularly when children are involved. Despite heated arguments, the couple prioritizes their shared role as parents and works together to protect their children from the conflict. Kindness and humility go a long way. They also acknowledge their imperfections and the need to keep improving their communication, showing that even when values diverge, respect and commitment to family can serve as a strong foundation.

STRATEGIES FOR DOING YOUR BEST

As I look over the stories I just told and the many other stories I have collected throughout my work and travels, I remind myself of the following commonalities or overarching universal lessons or goals.

Preserve Respect for the Relationship

Many stories emphasize a strong commitment to maintaining the relationship despite fundamental differences. Whether it's a business partnership, romantic relationship, friendship, or neighborly bond, the people involved prioritize the relationship itself, which acts as a foundation for navigating disagreements.

Choose Effective Means of Communication

The stories that I consider to have a successful outcome (establishing or maintaining a human connection) highlight the importance of calm, measured communication and active listening, maintaining a respectful dialogue, carefully choosing words and checking facts, deploying intellectual humility, and a controlled approach to communication.

Access Emotional Intelligence and Self-Awareness

Many people in potentially volatile situations display a high level of emotional intelligence, being mindful of their own reactions and those of others. They recognize the emotional toll on their partner and the importance of addressing emotions alongside rational arguments.

Identify a Unifying Shared Value or Goal

Despite differing views, there is often a shared value or goal that keeps the relationship intact.

Be Adaptable and Flexible

The ability to adapt to each other's perspectives and find points of connection is a recurring theme in interactions I've personally witnessed and those I've read about. People who can question their own beliefs, adapt their viewpoints to understand each other better, and agree on strategies to manage their disagreements (such as keeping debates private) have more positive outcomes.

AVOIDING ASSUMPTIONS

We all judge. Judging is natural and essential to human beings as a survival mechanism. It helped our ancestors determine trustworthiness and spot danger in unfamiliar situations, including encounters with other tribes or animals.

So, I am not asking us to stop doing what's natural to us. I also am not saying we need to agree with other people and accept their ideas just the way they are. Not at all. I am all for standing up for our morals, opinions, ways of thinking, and principles while respectfully disagreeing with others.

When I have judgmental thoughts, the one thing I *do not do* is to beat myself up over them. After all, as the famous psychiatrist Carl Jung said about judging,

"Thinking is difficult, that's why most people judge."

What I propose is to stay curious and open, even if for a short while, to postpone the judgment. What we are looking for is a compassionate and understanding mindset instead. The beginnings of compassion are rooted in our ability to notice that we are experiencing discomfort, put a name to the feelings, and express those emotions.

QUESTION YOUR ASSUMPTIONS TO TRULY SEE OTHERS

The stories we create about others, especially those different from us, often reveal more about our own assumptions than about their reality. I've seen this in my own life, from my initial judgments of Nicolas the baker who chose "enough" over expansion, to misinterpreting gestures and mannerisms. When we assume nothing, we open ourselves to genuine discovery rather than confirming what we already believe. Our first impressions almost never capture someone's full truth.

Practice assumption breaking through three simple moves that have transformed my relationships across divides: First, notice when you're filling gaps with stories ("They must be thinking this" or "They're clearly doing that because . . .") and catch yourself by asking curious questions instead. Second, look for evidence that might challenge your initial impression by wondering, "What else could explain this?" Finally, approach differences with genuine interest, saying things like, "I'm curious why you . . ." or, "Help me understand how you see this . . ." Your tone matters as much as your words, so soften your voice, maintain eye contact, and show through your whole presence that you're truly open to learning.

This week, notice someone you've made assumptions about, maybe a colleague whose approach differs from yours, a family member whose choices puzzle you, or someone from a different background. Before your next interaction, write down three assumptions you might be making, then create three open questions to explore these areas with curiosity instead of certainty. After your conversation, note what surprised you. What did you learn that you couldn't have guessed? How did questioning your assumptions change how you connected? I still remember how the residents in those Florida retirement communities revealed depths of wisdom I would have missed entirely if I'd held on to my initial judgments about their living arrangements. What might you discover when you set aside your assumptions and see others with fresh eyes?

Principle 3

LISTEN TO UNDERSTAND

*	State	Step 1	Step 2	Step 3
PRINCIPLE 3 **Listen to Understand**	Moving from Distracted to Understanding	Start with Awareness	Don't Just Listen—Hear	No Solutions Required

Moving from Distracted to Understanding

It was 2017, and I was in Paris for a business meeting with a potential investor for Les Lunes, my sustainable fashion company. After our formal discussions, we moved to a café for a more casual conversation. As we settled into our chairs, he mentioned casually that he didn't "believe" in climate change.

I nearly choked on my tea.

My company was built on sustainability principles. We sourced bamboo fabric specifically to reduce environmental impact. Our entire brand story centered on ethical, environmentally conscious fashion. And here was someone, educated, successful, seemingly rational, dismissing the very foundation of my company's mission.

My body reacted before my mind could catch up. My jaw tightened, my shoulders tensed, and I could feel heat rising to my face. Inside my head, a torrent of thoughts raced: How could anyone still deny climate science? Is he testing me? Should I end this meeting? Can I possibly work with someone who thinks this way?

I was about to launch into a passionate defense of climate science armed with all the facts and figures I'd collected over years of research for my business. But something stopped me. Perhaps it was the memory of my own journey from skepticism to understanding on other issues, or maybe it was simply curiosity about how someone I otherwise respected could hold such a different view.

Instead of arguing, I took a deep breath and asked, "Can you help me understand how you came to that conclusion?"

What followed was eye-opening. He didn't actually deny that the climate was changing or that human activity affected the environment. His skepticism centered on specific policy approaches and the economic models used to predict future impacts. He worried about how climate policies might affect developing economies and whether proposed solutions would create new problems. Some of his concerns, I realized, were ones I shared, although we drew different conclusions.

As I listened, truly listened, I discovered that what I'd initially thought of as a binary belief or disbelief in climate change was actually a complex web of values, priorities, and information sources. We weren't as far apart as I'd assumed, though significant differences remained.

Did I change his mind that day? No. Did he change mine? Not on the fundamental issue. But something more important happened: We found enough common ground to continue a respectful dialogue, one that eventually led to us working together despite our differences.

This conversation taught me powerful lessons about situations where I thought it would be impossible to understand the other person's point of view. First, what made understanding difficult wasn't just the content of our disagreement but my reaction to it: my immediate assumption that his position was irrational (refer back to Principle 2), the physical tension that blocked my ability to listen, my rush to categorize him. Second, asking questions and truly hearing the answers is what created understanding and progress.

Have you ever felt that profound difference between being listened to and being truly heard? I have. I vividly remember sitting across from a colleague in Shanghai, struggling to explain my vision for our company's future. Though he nodded along, his eyes darted to his phone, his posture remained rigid, and his responses felt mechanical. Contrast this with a conversation I had later that week with my business partner at the time, Hong Zhou, who put aside his notes, leaned forward slightly, and seemed to absorb not just my words but the emotions behind them.

The difference wasn't in what I said, it was in how they received it. One merely listened; the other truly heard me. Moments like these showed me something I've seen everywhere: Listening is a technical skill, but hearing is the key to loving conflict.

It would seem common knowledge that listening is a vital skill. We live in a world that rarely creates space for the art of listening. Our attention is constantly fragmented by notifications, by internal chatter, by the pressure to respond quickly rather than deeply. Most of us have never been taught how to listen. We think it's simple: stay quiet while another person speaks. But true listening, the kind that creates understanding and connection, requires much more than silence. A 2021 article in the *Harvard Business*

Review entitled "How to Become a Better Listener" says that listening to understand is rarely, if ever, explicitly taught as such (outside of training for therapists). While 78% of accredited undergraduate business schools list "presenting" as a learning goal, only 11% identified "listening."

So, it's not surprising that many of us do not listen well.

In business, this can lead to significant losses. For example, a team lead pushing his ideas without addressing *his team's concerns* may cause projects to derail due to unaddressed risks. An executive who talks more than they listen to clients can lose important deals because they are not seeing the big picture. In personal life, a parent not hearing his teenager can lead to emotional distance and unexpected alienation, and a friend who gives advice without fully listening may cause a strained relationship because they make the other person feel unvalued. In each case, missed listening leads to disconnection and missed opportunities.

Let's explore the true meaning of deep listening and how important it is for connecting with others.

LEARNING LISTENING IN CHINA

> There we were sitting around a big round table, me, a twenty-year-old, easily excitable, determined young entrepreneur, and ten older, serious Chinese men, the upper management of the factory whose partnership was critical to our young company's success. This first meeting would determine whether they would join our alliance of sustainable, ethical factories in China.
>
> We said our hellos; the tea was served. We smiled politely to each other. No one spoke. Not even me, even though I was bursting with ideas, passion, and plans for our partnership.

My business partner Hong Zhou looked at me reassuringly as if to say that everything was all right. Everyone kept silent. For what seemed like hours.

This was one of the hardest moments of my life. I don't know how you feel when you are with someone and there is a complete silence, but I was extremely uncomfortable. More time passed. We all just sat and sat, sipping our tea, looking at each other, in silence.

Then one of the men from the factory finally spoke. He announced that they were interested to hear what we had to propose.

That meeting ended up being a total success. We signed the deal, and that factory became our first partner in the long and successful endeavor of connecting high-quality, sustainable, and ethical manufacturers of China with the rest of the world. This project is still thriving, twenty-two years later.

But why the silence at the beginning?

Later on Hong Zhou explained: "In Chinese culture, when people wait to speak, whoever speaks first and shows more excitement for the deal ends up having less leverage in the negotiation."

As a young entrepreneur, I was eager to learn the skills of negotiation, and I wanted to know how to have more leverage. So, at that moment I made a commitment that I still keep today, twenty-two years later: I will practice staying silent, being comfortable with the silence in the room, and listening to the others instead. It's a vital skill for everyone, in business and in life in general.

Tea ceremonies and mah-jongg games in my early days in China taught me about presence and curiosity. Later, in a crucial business negotiation, China would offer perhaps its most valuable lesson yet: the power of silence and truly hearing beyond words. This moment of silence revealed more than hours of conversation I'd had elsewhere. In fact, during my twenty years in China, I mostly listened. This commitment to listening led me to understand the challenges facing Chinese manufacturers in the '90s and inspired me to create Streamline Alliance, connecting ethical Chinese manufacturers with Western companies committed to sustainability.

For twenty-two years now, that first business, Streamline Alliance, has been building a network of artisan and sustainable manufacturers who build high-quality products. We work with them to make sure they comply with all the necessary standards and regulations, and then find customers for them in the West who care about sustainability, ethics, and selling high-quality products. Long before this conversation became popular in the West, we started our commitment to ethical, sustainable production of high-quality products that last. This business is still very much thriving today *because* I listened to Hong Zhou and kept silent.

ARE YOU WILLING TO CHANGE YOUR MIND?

When speaking with groups of all types, I often challenge with the question of whether they listen willing to change their minds. I am met with a variety of reactions on their faces, surprise, shock, and sometimes even anger, when we start to discuss how to listen better. I think this is probably the hardest proposition I make in my workshops. For to truly listen well, to learn to use conflict constructively, we need to be willing to change our minds.

On the surface, this should seem a simple enough proposition to consider. After all, the opposite, listening to someone sharing their opinion while not being willing to reconsider ours, sounds totally unacceptable. Yet, surprisingly, this is how many people often listen. They appear to be in the conversation, but the whole time they are thinking about how to argue their point of view, how to masterfully (in their mind) disagree, and how to prove the other person wrong.

Obviously, this type of conversation doesn't go far. Because, in fact, it is not a conversation. If one or both participants are not listening, it is more of a lecture, where they take turns talking at each other. Because of this dynamic, participants usually stay entrenched in their points of view, remaining unmoved, because they feel equally unheard and unseen.

What I am after is another type of conversation. I am after the one where there is a feeling of being listened to, of being fully seen, acknowledged, and respected. It is that type of conversation that leads to understanding, connection, and possibly, a shift of ideas and opinions.

And that quality of conversation can only be achieved if we listen while being willing to change our minds. A willingness to change our minds may be the most challenging aspect of deep listening. Our beliefs and perspectives feel like part of our identity, and reconsidering them can be uncomfortable, even threatening. This is especially true in business contexts, where being "right" often seems crucial to success. But my experiences in China showed me that sometimes the greatest wisdom comes from allowing ourselves to be influenced by what we hear rather than holding rigidly to our preconceptions.

Creating the Conditions for Better Listening

I'll talk about specific actions you can take to become a better listener in the next three chapters, but here are four general guidelines to set the stage:

- **Create a mindful atmosphere.** For meaningful dialogue, establish calm, deliberate conditions. When triggered or hurried, we cannot remain open to different viewpoints. As Thich Nhat Hanh observed: "Mindfulness helps you go home to the present."

continued

- **Embrace intellectual humility.** As I discussed in Chapter 2, we have to acknowledge that we don't have all the answers and ensure we are open to learning from others, even when it challenges our preconceptions. Intellectual humility allows us to approach conversations with curiosity rather than defensiveness.

- **Focus purely on listening.** Truly engage with what the other person is saying, without immediately planning your rebuttal. This means focusing on understanding their perspective fully before responding.

- **Remember the conversation/negotiation/discussion is not a competition or debate.** Establish that the right goal for our conversations is to understand each other and learn something new, not to "win" an argument or prove who is smarter, more informed, or better prepared.

FACILITATING TRUE LISTENING

As you know by now, I am quite obsessed with listening well. And even though it often requires hard work, focus, full presence, and the ability to delay judgments and resist the urge to jump in, it pays off many times over. We all know how good it feels when we're truly being listened to. People describe it in different ways: like taking a deep breath, feeling grounded, being held tenderly, feeling loved for who they are, or simply feeling fully relaxed with no need to explain themselves. It's always a positive feeling.

And there's another side to the situation: It also feels incredibly rewarding to be the one listening. When I focus my full presence on someone, the connection that builds between us is palpable to me. I have a feeling of fulfillment that comes from knowing I've given someone the space to be themselves, without judgment, without rush.

In my work, I get to see people experience this feeling of being deeply listened to, and I can feel the impact it has on them. Some of my favorite moments are watching people relax and smile peacefully, knowing they've been truly heard. Seeing their expressions of relief and connection makes all the effort and practice worth it. Listening well benefits not only the person being heard but also the listener. It brings a sense of genuine collaboration that nourishes us both. *It feels incredibly rewarding to be the one listening.*

I still struggle with listening to understand. My mind races ahead, formulating responses before the other person has finished speaking. I catch myself half listening while planning my day or replaying earlier conversations. In moments of disagreement, I sometimes listen to find flaws rather than to understand perspectives. And when someone shares pain or struggle, I too quickly leap to offering solutions rather than simply holding space for their experience.

Yet I've also experienced the transformative power of being truly heard, those rare conversations where someone's complete attention makes you feel fully seen, where they seem to understand not just your words but the feelings and values behind them. These moments of deep listening create a singular kind of connection, one that bridges differences and fosters trust unlike anything else.

This principle builds directly on the foundations we've established. The presence we cultivated in Principle 1 creates the attentional space that listening requires. The practice of assuming nothing from Principle 2 frees us from prejudging what we'll hear, allowing us to listen with genuine curiosity. Now, with Principle 3, we apply these capacities to the art of listening for understanding.

The following chapters will walk you through the three steps of listening to understand:

	State	Step 1	Step 2	Step 3
PRINCIPLE 3 **Listen to Understand**	Moving from Distracted to Understanding	Start with Awareness	Don't Just Listen—Hear	No Solutions Required

- **Step 1: Start with awareness.** We start with awareness, noticing our own internal state and preparing ourselves to truly listen.

- **Step 2: Don't just listen—hear.** This is the core of Principle 3. Move beyond listening to truly hearing, absorbing not just words but emotions, values, and unspoken messages.

- **Step 3: No solutions required.** Create space without solutions, resisting the urge to fix or advise when what's needed is simply to witness and understand.

As with other actions recommended in this book, these steps may feel challenging at first. I still find myself slipping into old patterns: distractedly nodding while my mind wanders, or half listening while formulating my response. We're all simply practicing, learning this dance of human conflict and connection together.

What I've discovered is this: When we listen to understand, we create something rare. A space where people feel safe to reveal their truths, where we actually connect beyond our differences. We offer perhaps the greatest gift one human can give another: the experience of being truly heard.

Step 1

START WITH AWARENESS

	State	Step 1	Step 2	Step 3
PRINCIPLE 3 Listen to Understand	Moving from Distracted to Understanding	Start with Awareness	Don't Just Listen—Hear	No Solutions Required

In many cultures, speed has become a marker of success. We pride ourselves on how much we can pack into a single day, treating efficiency as though it's the only measure of achievement. But this relentless pace has a hidden cost, one I've observed most clearly in relationships and decision-making.

When we rush, we lose awareness of ourselves and the people around us. Conversations become hurried, shallow exchanges rather than meaningful dialogues. The potential for harmful conflict increases. Decisions made in haste are often disconnected from our values and long-term goals. The ability to truly listen gets drowned out in the noise of a life lived too fast.

Cultivating awareness is the antidote to this disconnection. By turning our attention inward, we can tune in to the subtle dynamics of our interactions: the emotions behind our words, the tension in our bodies, the unspoken messages in the room. Awareness grounds us, slows us down, and opens the door to deeper connections.

This emotional awareness builds directly on the emotional mastery we began cultivating in Step1.2. There, we learned to recognize how emotions like anger can reveal our values. Now, we're extending that awareness to create the internal conditions for truly hearing others. The better we understand our own emotional landscape, the more skillfully we can move through the emotions of our conversations.

RECLAIMING ATTENTION

I believe we need to reclaim our attention in a world constantly pulling it in a thousand directions. For me, this journey begins with turning my focus inward, really feeling what's happening in my body, noticing the patterns of my thoughts, and becoming fully present to my surroundings.

I've explored many paths to this deeper awareness over the years. During my time in California, I fell in love with yoga and discovered how my breath could anchor me when my mind wanted to race ahead. In China, I observed practitioners of Tai Chi in parks at dawn, their slow, deliberate movements embodying the very presence I was seeking. As I talked about in the opening to Principle 2, I loved living near the redwoods of Mill Valley where I hiked for hours simply immersing myself among the trees, letting their ancient stillness quiet the chatter in my mind.

What amazes me is that these aren't just nice philosophical ideas, these practices actually change our brains! I didn't realize it at the time, but all the hours I'd spent in meditation weren't just calming my mind.

They were literally reshaping my brain's architecture. The changes happen in fascinating places in the brain: the prefrontal cortex (which helps us plan and make decisions) and the hippocampus (crucial for memory and managing emotions).

I find it incredibly empowering to know that when I take time to cultivate awareness, I'm not just feeling different in the moment, I'm building lasting capacity for presence that supports me in all my relationships. My brain is actually becoming better at paying attention and regulating emotions with each practice session.

FACING THE INNER DIALOGUE

Slowing down is not just about physical awareness. It also means becoming aware of the thoughts that arise during challenging conversations, the fleeting, sometimes insistent mental whispers that shape how we engage. These are thoughts that run through my own mind, often uninvited, in the heat of dialogue:

- This is too uncomfortable.

- I don't care enough about this.

- You're wrong.

- This doesn't make sense.

- This is not like this for me. My experience is different.

- This sounds unreal. I don't believe you.

- You don't even like me. I don't even like you.

- This is too much for me. I can't take this on right now.

- What's the point of continuing this conversation?

It's fascinating to catch these uncomfortable thoughts and notice how they affect my ability to listen. For instance, when I feel discomfort or resistance, my body reacts: my shoulders tighten, my arms cross, or my breathing becomes shallow. These physical responses are signals of my inner state, and they often correspond with judgmental or dismissive thoughts.

Noticing these intrusive thoughts and their resulting physical sensations is a precious gift I've learned to give myself. It's the practice of tuning in to my inner world to better understand how it shapes my outer interactions. Especially in the middle of an uncomfortable conversation, recognizing these thoughts allows me to pause and reflect: What's really happening here? Why am I feeling this way?

What's really happening here? Why am I feeling this way?

Through mindfulness, I've learned that these thoughts are barriers to attentive listening. They create walls of judgment, defensiveness, and disengagement, which increase the potential for harmful conflict. If I'm thinking, "You're wrong," I'm not truly hearing the other person. If I'm overwhelmed with, "This is too much for me," I've already shut down emotionally.

These thoughts, left unchecked, take me out of the moment and away from the possibility of meaningful connection.

Instead of letting these disagreeable thoughts dominate, I've learned to acknowledge them without judgment. It's okay to feel uncomfortable or challenged, it's part of being human. When I catch myself thinking, "I don't believe you," I try to reframe it: What could that person be experiencing that I haven't considered? Shifting from judgment to curiosity creates space for empathy and understanding.

Letting go of these judgments, even temporarily, requires practice and vigilance. It's not about suppressing them but postponing their influence.

This mental discipline helps me focus on what matters: hearing the other person fully. By cultivating this awareness, I've discovered deeper presence in conversations, which allows me to use conflict as a catalyst for connection and understanding.

TECHNIQUES FOR CREATING AWARENESS

Remember my conversation with the person who had different views on climate change that I talked about in the previous chapter? That experience reminded me that we all have conversations or people that feel impossible to understand. The ones that leave us frustrated, confused, or even angry because the gap between their perspective and ours seems too vast to bridge.

I've since encountered many other "impossible to understand" scenarios: a family member whose political views felt worlds apart from my own, a close friend whose life philosophy seemed completely opposite to their actions, a colleague's approach to parenting that seemed unnecessarily harsh. In each case, the barrier to understanding wasn't just the difference in perspective but my own internal response: the judgment, tension, and assumptions that arose automatically. The limits of my own understanding often contributed to the tension, and awareness of my reactions was critical in lessening tension.

That's why awareness of these internal blocks has become my first step in moving from impossible to possible understanding. Now, when I encounter views that challenge me deeply, I try to notice:

- **My physical response.** Where am I feeling tension? How is my breathing changing?

- **My emotional reaction.** What emotions are arising? Fear? Anger? Confusion?

- **My assumptions.** What am I assuming about this person's intentions or reasoning?

- **My listening blocks.** Am I categorizing rather than staying curious? Preparing arguments rather than seeking understanding?

Simply noticing these reactions creates a crucial pause between stimulus and response where more thoughtful listening becomes possible. This doesn't mean suspending all judgment or accepting every viewpoint as equally valid. It means creating enough internal space to truly hear someone before deciding how to respond.

What I've discovered through these challenging encounters is that "impossible to understand" is often more about my own limitations than the other person's perspective. When I become aware of my internal obstacles to listening, what seemed impossible often becomes merely difficult, and what seemed difficult sometimes transforms into an opportunity for connection across difference.

> *"Impossible to understand" is often more about my own limitations than the other person's perspective.*

What's your "impossible to understand" scenario? And what happens when you bring awareness to your own internal response to it? The journey to understanding others begins not with their words, but with our awareness of how we receive them.

CONNECTING MIND AND BODY

Two other practices have been especially transformative for me in terms of creating greater awareness of what's going on with my body, physically and emotionally: the Alexander Technique and Vipassana meditation. You may find other techniques helpful for you, but I'd like to share my experiences with both these practices so you can understand the purpose and effect of learning to pay better attention to our bodies.

Experiences with the Alexander Technique

It was the winter of 2023, one of the coldest I can remember in recent years. Each week, I would bundle up and make my way to the eleventh arrondissement of Paris, to a modest ground-floor studio of a multistory apartment building in this busy neighborhood. This was where my instructor, a man in his seventies, guided me into the subtle yet transformative world of the Alexander Technique. The Alexander Technique is a method that teaches improved posture and movement, focusing on unlearning harmful physical habits and developing mindfulness of how we use our bodies in everyday activities.

Each session lasted two hours, a deep dive into slowing down and paying attention. The exercises seemed deceptively simple. One week, he asked me to pick up a glass of water, encouraging me to use only the muscles absolutely necessary for the task. Over and over, I reached for the glass, each time noticing just how much tension I carried in my shoulders, neck, and even jaw.

"Why are you working so hard?" he would ask gently, his voice a soothing contrast to my self-criticism. "Let go of what isn't needed."

Bit by bit, I became more attuned to my body. I began to notice not just the unnecessary tension in my movements but also how my emotions lived in my muscles. When I crossed my arms in discomfort, my teacher guided me to relax, uncross, and explore the openness that followed. I started to feel how my posture influenced my thoughts and vice versa.

By the end of each session, I felt lighter, as if my body and mind had been reset. But reentering the noisy, frenetic world outside the studio was always a shock. The cacophony of Paris, the screech of the metro, the chatter of pedestrians, the rumble of traffic, seemed unbearably loud. Every detail was magnified: the rush of cold air on my face, the rhythm of my footsteps on the pavement, even the weight of my coat pressing on my shoulders.

When leaving each session, I'd wonder, "How can I possibly take the metro now?" My heightened awareness felt like a double-edged sword, enriching but overwhelming. It wasn't until much later that I learned how to embrace this sensitivity without letting it consume me, how to notice everything and yet let it pass without clinging to it. Doing this now allows me to notice subtle cues in my own body, like crossing my arms when I feel uncomfortable or unnecessarily tensing my neck during moments of disagreement. These small physical reactions, though seemingly insignificant, can influence the energy of a conversation. Once I become aware of them, I have the choice to adjust: to uncross my arms, relax, or shift my posture.

I came to notice that these small adjustments often ripple outward. When I uncross my arms, my opponent sometimes mirrors the gesture, signaling a subtle opening to dialogue. Relaxing the tension in my neck often softens my facial muscles, which can lead to a more relaxed expression in the other person. These moments, though subtle, create a more receptive and open space for connection, enabling both sides to listen more attentively and respond more thoughtfully.

The Alexander Technique taught me about more than my body. It taught me how to be present in chaos without being consumed by it. When I find that stillness inside, everything gets easier. I can move through life with less effort and more intention.

Those sessions taught me awareness of my body: the subtle tensions, the unconscious habits, the physical signs of what I was feeling inside. But my journey into awareness was just beginning. Alexander showed me the body. Vipassana would show me the mind.

Vipassana: Slowing Down the Mind

In 2019, after selling my company Les Lunes, I attended my first ten-day silent Vipassana retreat in a meditation center in the lush jungles of New Zealand. It was an experience that redefined my relationship with time, silence, and awareness. Vipassana is an ancient Indian meditation technique that involves observing physical sensations and mental patterns with detached awareness, ultimately leading to insight into the nature of reality and oneself.

The retreat demanded total disconnection: no phones, no reading, no writing, no speaking. Days began at four a.m. with the resonant sound of a gong, pulling us into a schedule of long meditation sessions, only interrupted by several light meals and short, silent walks. The meditation hall, with its high, vaulted ceiling supported by beams of rich, aged wood, became a place of transformation.

At first, my mind fought back. Thoughts swirled, racing with unresolved questions and to-do lists. I questioned my decision to come, asking myself why I had chosen to spend ten days in silence when I could have been planning my next business. But as I settled into the rhythm of stillness, something remarkable happened.

The world around me came alive. The dense jungle symphony of rustling leaves, birdsong, and the hum of insects became vibrant and layered. The colors of the forest, vivid greens, fiery reds, and golden yellows, pulsed with life. Even the simple act of walking felt profound, as though my feet were discovering the earth for the first time.

But the real transformation happened inside. I began to notice my thoughts. Not just fleeting ones but deeply buried narratives about my identity, fears, and relationships. Some were painful, forcing me to confront moments I had avoided. Others brought clarity, helping me reevaluate what truly mattered.

Returning to my daily life, I was pleased to find that I carried my new-found awareness with me. Conversations became richer as I learned to pause and truly hear what others were saying. My relationships deepened, particularly with my parents and in-laws, as I gave them the space to express themselves without interruption or judgment.

Even the smallest rituals, like making my bed, became acts of mindfulness. What once felt mundane turned into opportunities to be fully present, to align my inner and outer worlds.

Inward Focus Creates Outward Connection

While very different in approach, the Alexander Technique (focused on physical posture and movement) and Vipassana (focused on observing our own minds) both taught me the art of paying exquisite attention. I discovered a beautiful paradox: *By turning our attention inward, we actually enhance our capacity to connect outward.* As I became more attuned to subtle shifts in my own body and mind, I naturally became more sensitive to these shifts in others.

Awareness, it turns out, is the foundation upon which all genuine connection is built. When we slow down enough to notice what's happening within us, we simultaneously become more available to truly hear what's happening in others.

THE POWER OF AWARENESS

Awareness is not just about slowing down; it's about developing a deeper relationship with ourselves. When we cultivate awareness, we gain the ability to notice our thoughts and sensations without being overwhelmed by them. We become more attuned to how our emotions show up in our bodies, how our judgments cloud our listening, and how our presence shapes the quality of our interactions.

This practice transforms the way we engage with others. By noticing when our arms are crossed or when judgmental thoughts creep in, we can consciously shift our posture, our mindset, and our responses. These changes de-escalate conflict and create space for more open, empathetic communication. Awareness also gives us resilience. In a world filled with noise and distractions, being attuned to ourselves allows us to stay grounded. We can navigate difficult conversations, chaotic environments, and unexpected challenges with greater clarity and intention.

Ultimately, cultivating awareness is an act of care not just for ourselves but for the people we interact with. It prepares us to listen fully, connect deeply, and build relationships rooted in understanding and respect.

DON'T JUST LISTEN—HEAR

	State	Step 1	Step 2	Step 3
PRINCIPLE 3 Listen to Understand	Moving from Distracted to Understanding	Start with Awareness	Don't Just Listen—Hear	No Solutions Required

What are the external signs of a good listener? How does the other person know they are truly being heard? This is especially important because, as I've touched upon earlier, we often move too fast in our conversations, rarely taking the time to confirm that real communication has occurred.

George Bernard Shaw once observed, "The problem with communication is the illusion that it has been accomplished." His statement resonates deeply with me, and I'm sure many of us have experienced this phenomenon, whether we were aware of it or not. Listening isn't enough. As we'll explore in this chapter, hearing—deep, intentional hearing—is the key to bridging gaps in communication.

LISTENING WITHOUT UNDERSTANDING

At one of the first companies I started in Shanghai, China, called Beacon Brand Management, we worked with Church's Chicken, a US fried chicken franchise looking to replicate KFC's success in the Chinese market. Their strategy relied on signing franchise deals to develop their brand in China. That meant finding the right franchisees, managing relationships, building a supply chain system, etc. My company's main role was to be a bridge between the two very different cultures, American and Chinese.

We found a perfect franchise partner for Church's Chicken in Shanghai: Mr. Zhang, a prominent restaurateur known for his chain of high-end Shanghainese cuisine. He wanted to expand his portfolio with an American fast-food brand and diversify his offerings for the growing middle class. Mr. Zhang was also eager to learn franchising systems from the inside.

After the master franchise agreement was signed, the process of building Church's fried chicken fast-food restaurants in Shanghai started. Training the franchisees, acquiring the equipment, setting up the operation, and arranging for franchisees to visit restaurants in other countries to learn from the existing models were all part of ensuring the consistency and success of the new model.

This particular visit was to the first restaurant. The team included the head of franchising visiting from the US, plus several other executives from the US head office, including the head of marketing and the CEO. Opening the first restaurant in China was a big deal!

When we entered the restaurant, we were greeted by Mr. Zhang himself, smiling proudly. He proceeded to show us how the restaurant customers were greeted at the door and led to be seated at the tables. He was very proud to point out that they did not have to line up to order and pay at the counter. They could sit down, be comfortable, order at the tables, and pay after.

Now remember, Church's Chicken is a fast-food restaurant concept. They pride themselves on their fast service, whether at the drive-through window or the counter. Ordering never takes place at the tables!

Then came another shock. On the menu, we noted some additions to the regular Church's fare of fried chicken, fries, and chicken sandwiches. Customers could order fried shrimp, morning porridge with preserved egg, and corn-and-pork soup.

First, we tasted the fried chicken. Unfortunately, it was cold. Since the system was set up per Church's model, the food was not designed to be served at a table, but rather in a box as takeout or eaten right away, not served on a nice open plate, where it could get cold.

Mr. Zhang acknowledged the problem and assured the executive team from the US that he would work it all out. He wanted to test some different concepts to see what might work best in the Shanghai market and then adjust accordingly. He already had a plan to address the temperature of the food. And he was excited to share how the additional menu items were selling two to three times more than Church's original menu items. Locals were used to local food staples and appreciated being able to be served at the table.

Seeing the disbelief, worry, and even anger on the faces of the US corporate managers, Mr. Zhang kept showing them data to see if he could change their minds.

Unfortunately, the franchiser team refused to listen to what Mr. Zhang was saying. They stormed out of the restaurant, angry about all the changes, and immediately started working with their lawyers to cancel the franchising agreement. Despite all our efforts to explain the honest intentions of the Chinese franchisee, this relationship failed. As a result, there is no Church's Chicken in China.

In fact, the experience of Church's leadership team in China contains many lessons about what *not* to do when it comes to listening and hearing:

- **They did not embrace intellectual humility.** The Church's executives, confident in the success of their fast-food model elsewhere, dismissed Mr. Zhang's local knowledge and data showing that table service and menu adaptations resonated with Shanghai consumers. Their lack of humility prevented them from recognizing the value of these changes. By contrast, KFC and Starbucks showed intellectual humility by trusting their local partners' expertise. They understood that what worked in the US would not necessarily work in China, and they adapted their operations accordingly, adding local menu items, redesigning store layouts, and embracing cultural nuances.

- **They were too focused on explaining their position instead of understanding what Mr. Zhang was saying.** Church's US team entered the Shanghai restaurant with preconceived notions of what their brand should look like and refused to engage with Mr. Zhang's explanations. Instead of listening to his data and reasoning with an open mind, they quickly planned their rebuttal, dismissing his efforts as deviations rather than potential improvements. KFC and Starbucks, on the other hand, focused on listening intently to local teams and data. By taking the time to truly understand consumer preferences, they identified opportunities to adapt their models in ways that both honored their brand and resonated with the Chinese market.

- **They treated the conversation as a competition.** Church's executives treated their discussions with Mr. Zhang as a battle to enforce their model rather than a dialogue to explore solutions. This adversarial approach led to frustration, a breakdown of trust, and ultimately the failure of the partnership. By contrast, KFC and Starbucks entered the Chinese market with the mindset that collaboration, not competition, was the key to success. They recognized that by learning from their local teams, they could build a model that worked for everyone involved.

- **They were not willing to change their minds.** In short, unlike KFC and Starbucks, Church's leadership refused to adapt, clinging to their original model despite compelling evidence that localization was working for other similar brands. The contrast is striking: KFC and Starbucks executives showed a willingness to change their minds based on local insights, while Church's rigidity led to their failure in the Chinese market, a powerful illustration of how openness to changing our minds directly impacts success.

Where could this shift your conversations? With family? Colleagues? Across any divide you face?

LISTENING TO NONVERBAL CUES

I learned something from psychologist Albert Mehrabian that confirmed what I'd experienced across different cultures. Our actual words account for only about 7% of how people receive our message. The rest comes from our tone of voice and body language. This explains why the phrase "I'm fine" can communicate the exact opposite depending on how we say it.

Here's a story that makes this point.

> While living with my family in Mill Valley, California, I had the privilege of sharing a home with Tsering, a Tibetan woman who grew up in India and had moved to the US for work. She became like a sister to me, and we shared an open and honest communication style.
>
> However, I quickly noticed something that puzzled me: Tsering would often shake her head in a way that I interpreted as a "no," even when her words clearly meant "yes."
>
> For instance: "Would you like to have breakfast together?" Tsering shook her head (instead of nodding) but then joined me at the table.
>
> "Will you be home late? Should I leave the door unlocked?" Another head shake, leaving me wondering whether it was a yes, no, or maybe.
>
> This was my first exposure to the Indian culture, and I was quite clueless and very curious.
>
> One day, I finally asked her to clarify. Her response opened my eyes to the complexity of nonverbal communication. The "Indian head shake," as I learned, can signify agreement, understanding, approval, or even polite hesitation, depending on the context. I later also understood that the same gesture can also be used in an intentionally vague manner, such as an unenthusiastic head bobble being a polite way of declining something without outright saying no.

Once I learned that, asking for clarification became even more important. In matters of sharing living spaces, eating together, and taking care of children as a team, clarity was a must. It was fascinating, and also a lesson in how vital it is to seek clarity, especially when gestures carry multiple meanings.

When I moved with my family across the ocean from San Francisco to Paris, I quickly realized how different the mannerisms of people here were compared to Californians. Even after fifteen years with my husband, Jerome, I am still deciphering many of the gestures he and others use in daily interactions.

One gesture that took me time to understand, and still surprises me, is the famous "French shrug." It's a subtle lift of the shoulders, sometimes accompanied by raised palms or a half shrug, and often delivered with a calm, almost detached expression. Every time Jerome does this during an important conversation, I make it a point to ask for clarification.

"I notice you're shrugging," I'll say. "Are you disagreeing? Do you think what I'm saying isn't important? Or do you just need more time to think it over?"

You might wonder if this level of attention to a gesture is overkill. Why not just keep talking and figure it out? I've tried that approach, and it failed miserably. Because of my cultural heritage, to me, shrugging feels dismissive, like a silent rejection of what's being said or the person saying it. When I feel dismissed, even unintentionally, it disrupts our communication and connection. So, I persist in seeking clarity, and I'm glad I do.

Over time, I've come to understand the complexity of the "French shrug." It can convey resignation, indifference, a lack of knowledge or certainty, or simply an attitude of *c'est la vie* (such is life). It's deeply ingrained in French culture, reflecting a relaxed acceptance of things beyond one's control or deemed inconsequential. In Jerome's case, I've learned that his shrug often signals he's taking time to think something over, rather than dismissing me or the topic.

This seemingly small gesture holds an entire world of meaning, reminding me how essential it is to clarify nonverbal cues, especially in multicultural relationships. Each culture has its own shorthand, its own way of expressing subtleties, and when those signals go unexamined, misunderstandings can multiply.

Nonverbal cues are another critical part of listening. Often, these can be subtle or culturally specific, making them easy to misinterpret. It's essential to notice and clarify them. This can transform potential misunderstandings into opportunities for deeper understanding.

WHY CLARIFYING NONVERBAL CUES MATTERS

Here's something I've learned about communication. When someone's words don't match their body language, we believe the body. Psychologist David Matsumoto's research shows that when verbal and nonverbal messages conflict, most of the information we take away comes from the nonverbal signals.

We pick up on these cues even when we're not aware of it. You leave a meeting feeling uneasy without knowing why. Later you realize their crossed arms, minimal eye contact, and tight facial expressions were signaling discomfort. You registered it but didn't consciously process it in the moment.

This is why I've learned to trust that vague sense that something isn't right. If you feel it, take the extra step to find out why. Ask. Clarify. Don't ignore what your body is telling you about what their body is saying.

This matters everywhere, not just across cultures. Research shows that up to 70% of international ventures fail due to communication barriers, but I bet you've seen the same thing happen between colleagues in the same office, family members at the same dinner table, partners in the same bed. Not lack of expertise or resources, but the inability to bridge gaps in nonverbal communication.

Two sides think they're agreeing, but their bodies are telling different stories. By the time anyone speaks up, trust is already damaged.

TECHNIQUES FOR HEARING BEYOND LISTENING

Really hearing what someone is telling us is a skill just like others I've talked about in this book. And as such it requires specific techniques and practice. Here are several practices for you to try.

Say It Again

One of the most effective ways to show that you are truly hearing someone is by reflecting back what you've understood. Whether through direct repetition or thoughtful paraphrasing, this practice reassures the speaker that their words have landed. It makes them feel seen, valued, and understood. When this step is skipped, the speaker may hesitate to share further details, and we risk missing key pieces of the conversation.

How do you do this? Paraphrase what you believe the other person has said to ensure understanding and to show that their perspective is valued. Express what resonates with you.

Set the Scene

Creating the right environment for deep listening is essential. A quiet room, comfortable seating, or whatever you need to be able to focus fully. Minimize any internal and external disruptions and distractions. Silence all the rings and pings. I've ritualized this process by asking those around me to turn their phones to silent mode and remove them from sight when we're together. Whether it's at business meetings, family dinners, or moments with my children, this simple act ensures that we are fully present.

I found that it's extremely important when listening to do just that: listen. I try hard to not interrupt the speaker or start formulating my counterargument while the other person is speaking. Instead, I keep reminding myself to focus entirely on their words. I speak up only if I lose focus or don't understand something, asking the speaker to repeat what they said. Not only does this show my dedication to understanding, but it also strengthens trust.

The Body Language Check-In

Nonverbal cues often carry more weight than words themselves, yet most of us scan right past them without conscious awareness. I've learned to create intentional moments during conversations to tune into what someone's body is telling me, to notice when their physical presence doesn't match their words.

Here's how I practice this: Every few minutes during important conversations, I do a quick mental scan. Are their shoulders tense? Is their posture open or closed off? Are they making eye contact? When I sense that disconnect between words and body language, I gently check in: "I'm hearing you say you're excited about this project, but something in your posture makes me wonder if you have concerns. Am I reading that right?"

What I've learned is that you don't need to become an expert at reading every gesture. You just need to notice when something feels off and find the courage to ask about it. In my work, I've watched people discover how much changes when they simply say, "I'm sensing something here. Can you help me understand?"

THE ART OF TRUE HEARING

During a "Loving Conflict" workshop in Chicago, I paired two executives from the same company who had been avoiding each other for months. One was a vocal supporter of stricter immigration policies, the other an advocate for more open borders. The tension between them was palpable. Everyone in the room could feel it.

I introduced them to what I call the "mic drop listening exercise," where one person speaks while the other can only listen. The listener's job is simple: understand the person behind the position.

What happened next still gives me chills. The immigration restrictionist shared that his grandfather had come to America with nothing and worked three jobs to build a life. He was afraid that if immigration became too easy, it would devalue the sacrifice his family had made. The open-borders advocate shared that his parents had fled violence and almost didn't make it to safety. He was afraid that restrictive policies would condemn other families to the violence his own had escaped.

After twenty minutes of this deep listening, the tension in their voices changed. They weren't debating immigration policy anymore. They were two grandsons honoring their families' courage while trying to figure out how to help other families find safety and opportunity.

They still disagreed about policy details. But they stopped being enemies and became collaborators trying to solve the same problem from different starting points.

The ultimate goal of listening is to ensure that the other person knows they are being heard. This requires shifting the spotlight away from ourselves and fully embracing the speaker's words. When I practice this, I make it a point to help the speaker feel at ease, show my enthusiasm for their thoughts, and encourage them to share fully. For that moment, *they* are the most important person in the room, not me.

The stories of Tsering's head shakes and Jerome's shrugs showed me something: True listening goes beyond words. It requires patience, curiosity, and a willingness to embrace what is unfamiliar or unexpected. When we make the effort to truly hear the other person, both their words and their unspoken messages, we unlock the potential for deeper understanding.

Step 3

NO SOLUTIONS REQUIRED

	State	Step 1	Step 2	Step 3
PRINCIPLE 3 Listen to Understand	Moving from Distracted to Understanding	Start with Awareness	Don't Just Listen—Hear	**No Solutions Required**

Like a lot of people, I have a natural tendency in conversations to offer my opinion, advice, and input. But my experiences in different cultures and contexts showed me that sometimes the greatest gift we can offer is our undivided attention without the need to fix, solve, or advise.

Our rush to offer solutions often comes from good intentions. We want to ease suffering, share our wisdom, or provide value to the conversation. But this impulse can actually interrupt the very connection we're trying to build. Why do we often fall victim to the urge to offer solutions to someone who is sharing with us, and how can we resist that urge?

RUSHING TO SOLUTIONS
CREATES BARRIERS TO CONNECTION

In my experience, when people rush to solutions, they unintentionally create the potential for conflict by creating barriers to connection: doing so shifts attention from the speaker's experience to the listener's thoughts about it. Offering solutions implies the speaker's feelings need "fixing" rather than witnessing; we miss deeper layers of what they're sharing, and we deprive them of discovering their own wisdom. As Brené Brown notes, responses like "At least . . ." or "Have you tried . . ." often shut down connection rather than deepen it. "Rarely can a response make something better," she says. "What makes something better is connection."

Similarly, psychologist Carl Rogers, pioneer of client-centered therapy, found that people grow most in environments where they feel deeply heard without judgment or direction. His research showed that the simple act of reflective listening, mirroring back what someone has shared without trying to steer them, created the conditions for profound personal insight and change.

This doesn't mean advice is never appropriate. There are certainly times when guidance is needed and welcomed. But even then, solutions are most effective after understanding has been established. As Stephen Covey wisely observed, "Seek first to understand, then to be understood."

In my own life, I've experienced the transformative power of being listened to without immediate solutions. During a particularly challenging period with my company, a mentor simply sat with me as I processed my fears and concerns. She didn't offer strategies or platitudes. Just questions that helped me explore my own thinking more deeply. I left that conversation with greater clarity not because she solved my problems, but because her attentive presence helped me hear myself more clearly.

The practice of listening without solving requires patience and restraint. It means sitting with discomfort, both theirs and ours, without rushing to relieve it. It invites us to trust that people often have the resources they need within themselves, and our role is to create the space where those resources can emerge.

This doesn't mean passive listening. We can still ask thoughtful questions, reflect back what we're hearing, and express empathy. But we do so with the intention of deepening understanding rather than directing outcomes.

The gift of this solution-free listening is profound. It honors the other person's agency and wisdom. It creates space for emotional processing that quick fixes often bypass. And perhaps most importantly, it offers the rare experience of being fully witnessed, an experience that is itself healing.

When we set aside our need to solve problems, something remarkable happens: We create space not just for the other person's thoughts, but for our own minds to shift and grow. It transforms listening from a passive activity into a dynamic exchange where both people have the opportunity to evolve.

This type of listening isn't just a technique; it's a stance toward human connection that recognizes our shared humanity. It says: "I trust your capacity. I honor your journey. I'm here not to fix you but to understand you." Those messages alone can reduce the potential for conflict.

> *"I trust your capacity. I honor your journey. I'm here not to fix you but to understand you."*

TECHNIQUES FOR DEVELOPING
LISTENING RESTRAINT

My husband, Jerome, is an incredibly smart man with a wealth of life and business experience. People reach out to him for advice on a daily basis. As CEO of a fast-growing, global high-tech startup, a three-time successful founder, and an engaged community and humanitarian donor and organizer, Jerome's advice is both valuable and helpful. Naturally, he's used to sharing his opinions and insights.

However, when we talk as husband and wife, most of the time I'm not asking for his advice. What I need is connection. I want to be heard, seen, understood, and witnessed. It took us both a bit of time to understand this: for me to clearly request listening from Jerome, and for Jerome to learn to keep his advice to himself until I explicitly ask for it.

Now, to make our talks work, Jerome often keeps a notebook with him so he can write down his ideas as they come up. That way, he doesn't have to blurt them out in the moment; instead, he gives me his best listening first. Then, when I'm ready and willing to hear it, he shares his thoughts and observations.

What I try to emphasize in my work is that the goal of interactions like these should always be to fully understand the other person. Generic problem-solving won't achieve that goal, and it may even be counterproductive. The other person might shut down, feel unheard, or disconnect from the conversation. When someone just needs to be heard, an unwanted solution can feel dismissive and alienating, no matter how well-intentioned it might be.

The more advice we give, the more power we may think we gain, but the more power we gain, the worse our listening ability gets.

So, when you are listening to someone, resist the urge to jump into problem-solving mode unless you're specifically asked. And even if you are asked, take some time to understand the issue fully before giving advice.

Avoid the temptation of dispensing a generic, off-the-cuff solution that doesn't have a personal connection to the matter you're discussing.

You can try sharing a personal experience that resonates with the issue at hand. If a colleague tells you they're nervous about an upcoming client presentation, don't immediately tell them what they "should" do. Before saying, "You should do this," or, "If I were you, I would . . ." try sharing a similar moment from your own experience. For instance, tell them, "I remember feeling the same before a big presentation. I was really nervous, and it was tough. What helped me was practicing in front of a friend and focusing on breathing. I wonder if any of that might help you? What usually helps you calm down when you're nervous?" These carefully chosen words help make the interaction more personal and authentic. It shows you're truly listening and understanding, rather than just offering canned advice.

Deep Listening Can Lead to Acknowledging Hard Truths

Sometimes loving conflict means discovering hard truths. I learned this when I tried to help two business partners who were stuck in constant conflict about their company's direction. I was convinced that if they could just hear each other's perspectives, they might find a path forward.

I was wrong.

The deeper they listened, the more clearly they heard how fundamentally different their visions had become. One partner wanted to scale rapidly and take big risks. The other wanted to grow slowly and preserve what they'd built. Through our listening exercises, they weren't finding a way forward together. They were discovering just how incompatible their dreams were.

continued

The listening didn't bring them together. It helped them realize they needed to part ways cleanly rather than continuing to fight about it. Sometimes loving conflict means discovering that collaboration isn't possible and that separation is the most caring choice.

They dissolved their partnership three months later, but they did it with respect and without destroying their friendship. The deep listening hadn't saved their business, but it had saved their relationship.

Not every conflict is meant to end in collaboration. Sometimes loving conflict means loving people enough to let them go.

LISTENING: FROM TECHNIQUE TO WAY OF BEING

My relationship with listening has evolved from seeing it as a skill to recognizing it as a stance toward human connection. What began as an effort to hear better has become a commitment to be fully present, a commitment I renew with each conversation.

Through practicing the three elements of deep listening—cultivating self-awareness, truly hearing beyond words, and resisting the urge to solve—I've discovered that listening is not passive but deeply active. It requires more energy, attention, and courage than speaking ever does. Perhaps this is why it remains countercultural in a world that celebrates quick responses and ready solutions.

I've discovered that listening is not passive but deeply active. It requires more energy, attention, and courage than speaking ever does.

Many of my experiences have revealed to me that the quality of our listening directly shapes the quality of our connections. As we move to Principle 4, The Art of Questioning, we'll explore how thoughtful inquiry builds on this foundation of deep listening. When we truly hear others, we earn the right to ask questions that matter, questions that open new paths to understanding rather than merely confirming what we already believe.

LISTEN TO UNDERSTAND, NOT TO RESPOND

When we truly hear someone, we create a space where conflict can turn into collaboration. Throughout my journey, I've noticed how often we listen while planning our response rather than truly receiving what's being shared. Real collaboration happens not when we have the perfect answer, but when we're fully present with another person's experience.

Practice deep listening through three simple moves that have helped me with even the most challenging conversations:

1. First, ground yourself physically, feeling your feet on the floor and taking a deep breath, just as I did before those intense Hope meetings.

2. Next, when the other person speaks, notice when your mind starts jumping ahead to solutions or counterpoints (we all do this), and gently bring your attention back to them.

3. Finally, resist the urge to fill silences or solve problems. Instead, reflect what you've heard and simply ask, "Is there more?"

This week, choose one conversation where you typically find yourself thinking about what to say next while the other person is still speaking. It might be with a colleague, family member, or friend whose perspective challenges you. For just that conversation, commit to listening without planning your response. After, take a moment to write down the answers to these questions: What did you notice that you might have missed before? Did anything surprise you? How did the quality of your attention affect what happened between you? Notice how being fully present, even without clever responses, creates deeper connection than any words could.

Reassurance: "What If They Don't Listen Back?"

One of the most common concerns I hear is: "What if I do all this work to understand them, but they never do the same for me? Am I just setting myself up to be used?"

I've felt this too.

Here's what I've learned. When you listen deeply to someone, you're not doing it to get the same in return. You're doing it because it changes you. It makes you less reactive, more grounded, more curious about what's really happening.

Sometimes the other person starts listening better because you're modeling it. Sometimes they don't. But when you truly understand someone, even if they never fully understand you, the dynamic still shifts. You stop being triggered by their reactions because you see where they're coming from.

You can listen deeply and still set boundaries. You can understand someone completely and still disagree with them. The skill serves you, regardless of what the other person does with it.

THE ART OF QUESTIONING

	State	Step 1	Step 2	Step 3
PRINCIPLE 4 **The Art of Questioning**	From Defensive to Interested	Be Deliberate	Ask the Interested Question	Question Together

From Defensive to Interested

The previous principles have prepared us to ask questions that open doors rather than close them. Questions born not from defensiveness but from genuine interest in understanding others. The presence we cultivated in Principle 1 creates the attentional space that thoughtful questioning requires. The practice of assuming nothing from Principle 2 helps us approach questioning with genuine curiosity rather than a hidden agenda. And the deep listening we practiced in Principle 3 ensures we're asking questions that respond to what's actually being said rather than to our own internal dialogue. Let's dive more deeply into these ideas about questioning.

QUESTIONING THE STATUS QUO

When I lived in California between 2009 and 2021, I was frustrated by the fashion choices that seemed available to me as a successful executive. I could either look like a mini-man in a suit or wear comfortable outfits that were much too casual for the boardroom. It also frustrated me that there were very few fashion brands that were made in sustainable and ethical ways. What I saw around me was that fast fashion seemed to be the status quo and the way to succeed in the fashion industry. But I wondered, "What if we experiment with a different way of doing fashion?"

And that was how my company Les Lunes was born. My own sustainable fashion brand would make apparel for men and women made from bamboo. Les Lunes became a vertically integrated global company spanning the US, France, and China. As I look back, I now think of it fondly, like a child who has grown up and embarked on its own successful journey.

In the beginning at Les Lunes, we learned how hard it is to run a truly ethical and sustainable fashion business. At every turn, every step, we faced what was an almost impossible challenge to do things sustainably, when it came to replacing plastic packaging, sourcing eco-friendly fabrics, or minimizing packaging in shipping. But we kept questioning and faced every challenge and "impossibility" and as a result, we grew individually and as a team.

We wanted to create fashion that had it all, functionality, comfort, flattering silhouettes, elegance, and appeal, and was made sustainably. To accomplish that, we were forced to question the fundamental design process itself.

Designing in our Parisian offices, while merely imagining what customers wanted, wouldn't suffice. As a result of this questioning, we decided to involve our customers directly in the design process.

Led by the amazing Melanie Viallon, our French design team spent time with a set of customers in San Francisco, in their homes, their bedroom closets, and their wardrobes. The team followed them throughout an average day, learning about their lifestyles, what they needed, and what support and delight they wished for from their clothes. The result of such an intense design process was totally worth the effort. We cherished witnessing our customers emerge from the store's dressing rooms, feeling rewarded and thrilled: "It feels amazing, as if it was made specifically for me!" And, of course, it was.

We also had to question how garment production was traditionally done. Instead of the usual conveyor-belt operation, where each person performs only one task all day long without seeing the whole garment, we decided to set up our factory in China emulating the way artisanal workshops are run. One worker crafted an entire garment from beginning to end. Our employees felt the satisfaction and pride that comes from creating a beautiful, high-quality product, and knowing that their creation was going to make someone happy.

I am deeply grateful for all the learning that came from questioning the design approaches and production models at Les Lunes. But our questioning extended to many other aspects of the business as well. Some additional challenges we tackled included:

- How could we eliminate unnecessary waste in our packaging? (Answer: We invested in sustainable packaging.)

- How could we prioritize timeless designs over fast fashion trends? (Answer: We created versatile pieces that customers could wear for years.)

- How could we ensure transparency and ethics throughout our supply chain? (Answer: We built strong relationships with suppliers and conducted audits to maintain high ethical standards.)

In the end, each obstacle became an opportunity for learning and growth. And it wasn't just the business that transformed, it was all of us, shaped by the questions we dared to ask.

QUESTIONING EVERYTHING

When I was growing up, my father instilled in me the value of questioning everything, the status quo, authority, and even my own assumptions. He had told me explicitly not to reveal our Jewish identity at school. In questioning his instruction, in following my own internal compass despite his caution, I was paradoxically practicing what he had taught me: "Question everything and everyone. Don't follow the status quo." Even authority figures we respect most deserve our thoughtful questioning, not our blind obedience.

The Les Lunes story taught me that questioning isn't about disrupting or proving points. It's about exploring possibilities and connecting more deeply with others. When done thoughtfully, it creates change without defensiveness.

It's okay not to have all the answers. Genuine curiosity opens doors you never knew existed.

Les Lunes was just one example of how I embraced the art of questioning and it became a way of life for me, permeating many aspects of my personal and professional development. I went on to question my spiritual and personal growth by learning mindfulness and meditation in the Vipassana community and at Spirit Rock Meditation Center. This questioning led me to become more deliberate in my thoughts and actions, and to become kinder to myself and others.

I questioned my relationship with my body and learned to appreciate and care for it within the body-positive community of pole dancing at Sisters in Motion SF. This journey helped me fall back in love with my body after having three children and witnessing its changes. I am now stronger and healthier than I have ever been due to this practice.

I questioned the role I played in my community by joining EO (Entrepreneurs' Organization), a global peer-to-peer network of founder CEOs where members volunteer to support each other's learning, growth, and well-being. As an introvert, I enjoy spending time alone. Becoming an EO member, I explored how an introvert can participate, support, and lead others while balancing the need for solitude.

FINDING YOUR FRANK: FRIENDS WHO HELP US QUESTION AND GROW

Questioning is hard work, and even harder to do alone. Luckily, I've had people in my life who help me practice this skill, including my good friend Frank.

> Frank is not just a close friend of mine; he's the one who always tells me the truth no matter how hard it might be to hear. He's German, originally from Cologne, and after Madrid, Sydney, and Hamburg, now lives in Berlin. He's a talented artist and photographer, a creative leader with impeccable taste and style. Imagine a tall, elegant man in a linen suit, bright red sneakers, and a Leica camera slung over his shoulder. He's sharp, confident, and thoughtful. A philosopher with a firm voice and a love for high-resolution music tracks.

For more than fifteen years, we've shared countless conversations. These aren't casual chats; they're full-speed debates where every idea is examined. Frank doesn't accept "Because that's how I feel" as an answer. He demands excellence in thought processing, argumentation, and idea presentation, clarity, precision, and thoughtful reasoning. Always eloquent and with well-thought-through ideas, Frank demands the same from others.

Frank has a unique ability to spot things I miss and challenge my ideas. And trust me, it's not always easy and often gets uncomfortable. Sometimes I leave our conversations feeling like a student who needs to redo her homework. But Frank's humor softens the discomfort, helping me turn those moments into opportunities for growth.

I remember one particular evening in San Francisco that perfectly captured Frank's role in my life. I had just developed a new business idea and was brimming with excitement. After weeks of brainstorming, I was certain I had created something revolutionary. Frank happened to be visiting from Berlin, and I couldn't wait to share it with him.

We met at a small café overlooking the Bay, where I spread out my hastily prepared business plan with barely contained pride. "This is it," I declared. "I think it's going to disrupt the entire industry."

Frank ordered a craft beer for himself and tea for me, carefully placed his Leica on the table, and began reading through my notes. The minutes stretched into hours as he methodically worked through my business plan, occasionally making notes in the margins. I fidgeted with my teacup, simultaneously eager for and dreading his assessment.

Finally, as the evening fog rolled in over the Bay, Frank put down my business plan and looked up at me. His face was serious. "Anna," he said, "let's be clear. This isn't ready. There's one good idea buried under a pile of assumptions."

My heart sank. I had been expecting praise, validation, excitement. Instead, Frank spent the next two hours deconstructing my entire idea. He started with a simple "Why?" After I answered, he asked "Why?" again. And then a third time, until I was forced to dig down to the real purpose behind my idea.

"Who exactly is this for?" he pressed. "Be specific. Not just 'busy professionals,' which professionals? What specific problem of theirs are you solving?"

"What makes you uniquely qualified to solve this problem?" he continued. "And why would someone pay for this instead of the five other solutions already on the market?"

"Where's your evidence that this is actually a problem people want solved? Have you interviewed potential customers? How many?"

What followed was a full-speed debate that lasted well into the night. Frank didn't accept "Because I feel it will work" or "I'm really excited about it" as answers to any of his critiques. He demanded excellence in thought processing, argumentation, and idea presentation, clarity, precision, and thoughtful reasoning. By midnight, my business plan was covered in notes, arrows, and questions.

I left that evening feeling both devastated and strangely energized. Frank had dismantled my idea, yes, but he had also shown me a path forward. His humor as we parted, "Next time, maybe start with something easier, like solving climate change," softened the blow and reminded me why his friendship was so valuable.

I spent the next three months completely reworking the business concept, conducting customer interviews, building a prototype, and developing a realistic financial model. When Frank reviewed the new version, his simple nod and "Now this has legs" was exactly the encouragement I needed to move forward with confidence.

Frank excels at three things:

- **Seeing the unseen.** He spots my blind spots and helps me see what I've missed.

- **Stress-testing ideas.** Whenever I have a new idea, Frank challenges it until only the strongest parts remain.

- **Opening my mind.** Frank questions my certainties, making me more open-minded and adaptable.

I am deeply grateful for Frank. He has made me a better thinker, a better friend, and a better person.

How Friends Help Us Question and Grow

True friends like Frank are like mirrors that reflect parts of us we might not otherwise see. They sharpen our perspectives, challenge our assumptions, and help us recognize what we might overlook. Through their honesty and insights, they encourage us to grow and learn.

Here's how friends can help us evolve our beliefs:

- **Provide honest feedback.** True friends point out what we might be missing or where we're holding on to ideas that no longer serve us. Their constructive feedback helps us reevaluate and grow.

- **Encourage open discussion.** Those deep, open-ended conversations where no thought is off-limits can clarify our opinions and stimulate our curiosity. These dialogues also help us stand strong when dangerous or harmful ideas gain influence around us. Clarifying our beliefs during these discussions equips us to discern truth from manipulation and misinformation. This clarity becomes a shield, empowering us to hold our ground against divisive narratives. Friends who encourage open discussions not only help us expand our perspectives but also strengthen our critical thinking.

- **Create space for vulnerability.** Trustworthy friends provide an environment where we can explore doubts and admit uncertainties without fear of judgment. This courage to be vulnerable is essential for growth.

- **Explore new perspectives.** Friends from diverse backgrounds, cultures, and beliefs expose us to new ways of thinking. This diversity of thought encourages us to question our own beliefs and consider alternative perspectives, enriching our understanding of the world.

These different ways friends help us grow, providing feedback, encouraging discussion, creating safe spaces, and bringing new perspectives, all work together to expand our understanding of ourselves and the world. They help us see around blind spots we might never discover on our own.

Who Is Your Frank?

I've shared how Frank has helped me grow through his honesty and questions. But who is your Frank? Who challenges you to think deeper, question more, and become the best version of yourself? Take a moment to think about the people in your life who help you grow. And if you don't have a "Frank," consider how you might find one or how you might become one for someone else. Start by noticing who makes you feel both cared for and stretched. Look for someone who listens deeply, asks thoughtful questions, and isn't afraid to challenge you with kindness. It might be a colleague, a friend, a mentor, or even someone you've only just met but feel curious about. And if no one comes to mind, try initiating deeper conversations with the people around you. Ask them what they think about something that matters to you, and really listen.

It's not always comfortable to have your ideas challenged, but it's worth it. With the right friends by our side, questioning becomes less daunting and more empowering. Together, we can uncover new perspectives, challenge outdated beliefs, and grow into more thoughtful, compassionate, and open-minded people.

While Frank helps me question on a personal level, this deliberate approach to questioning extends to all our interactions. When we slow down and choose our questions carefully, we create the conditions for genuine understanding. But the quality of our questions matters just as much as our approach to asking them.

THE IMPORTANCE OF QUESTIONING LONG-HELD BELIEFS

Imagine living in a world where you never question anything, accepting every belief and tradition as absolute truth. It might feel safe, like a warm, well-worn blanket, but it's a recipe for intellectual stagnation. My friend Frank makes sure I don't do this.

Constantly questioning our long-held beliefs is like keeping a window open for fresh air. It prevents us from becoming trapped in outdated ideas and helps us grow, both personally and intellectually. Think of the Renaissance, a time when thinkers like Petrarch and Erasmus dared to challenge the status quo. Petrarch, often called the "father of humanism," emphasized the value of questioning traditional knowledge and seeking wisdom through classical texts. Erasmus, a scholar of the Reformation, critiqued religious dogma and advocated for intellectual freedom and moral reform. Their willingness to question long-held beliefs sparked a revolution in thought, leaving a legacy that continues to inspire critical thinking today.

The Renaissance thinkers remind us that questioning is not about tearing things down; it's about building something better. It's human nature to cling to our beliefs, even when evidence contradicts them. This is called *belief perseverance*, and it can blind us to new perspectives. To grow, we need to overcome this tendency and embrace new information with an open mind. And critical thinking is our most valuable tool. It's not about doubting for the sake of doubting. It's about carefully evaluating evidence, being open to changing our minds, and enriching our understanding of the world.

HOW TO BECOME MASTER OF QUESTIONING

I admit that questioning can be intimidating and feel unnatural at times. When we question deeply held beliefs, it often triggers discomfort and defensiveness because such questions challenge core aspects of identity or long-standing assumptions. Past experiences influence this too: If someone has faced ridicule for challenging the status quo, they'll hesitate to do so again. Cultural norms also play a role; in some environments, conformity is valued over curiosity, making questioning seem disruptive.

In the following chapters, I'll describe the three steps you can take to become a master of the art of questioning:

*	State	Step 1	Step 2	Step 3
PRINCIPLE 4 The Art of Questioning	From Defensive to Interested	Be Deliberate	Ask the Interested Question	Question Together

- **Step 1: Be deliberate.** This focuses on being deliberate with our questions: slowing down, choosing our words carefully, and establishing rituals that support meaningful inquiry.

- **Step 2: Ask the interested question.** Ask genuinely interested questions, the kind that break down walls rather than build them.

- **Step 3: Question together.** Expand our questioning from an individual practice to a collective one, learning to question together in ways that deepen connection and understanding.

Recognizing these dynamics has helped me approach questioning with more empathy and care. This isn't about forcing others to see things my way; it's about gently inviting them to explore new ideas together. Through respect and compassion, we can foster more meaningful dialogues, even when challenging the status quo. That is why questioning everything thoughtfully and respectfully is so vital. This is as much a practice as the skills of staying open-minded and curious or listening to understand.

Step 1

BE DELIBERATE

	State	Step 1	Step 2	Step 3
PRINCIPLE 4 The Art of Questioning	From Defensive to Interested	Be Deliberate	Ask the Interested Queston	Question Together

In the discussion of Principle 3 about listening, we discussed slowing down so that we can take stock of our bodies, pay attention to our feelings, and check our thoughts and possible preconceptions. The same ideas apply to the art of questioning. But before going there, I want to talk about a question that went unasked.

THE QUESTION UNASKED

Maksym is a Ukrainian cameraman from Kyiv who moved to San Francisco in late 2021 to work for a US media company. He operated the camera during a TV interview I participated in and approached me afterward, something he said he rarely does with guests. The discussion on fostering respectful connection and listening had struck a chord with him, especially the idea that we can learn and practice how to have difficult or controversial conversations without losing empathy and respect.

Maksym's mind flashed back to February 2022, when Russia invaded Ukraine. At work, where he was one of the few Eastern Europeans on the team, he felt deeply uncomfortable and even scared. People around him either tiptoed around the conversation entirely or expressed strong opinions about the war, yet never actually asked him how he felt.

He found the same awkward distance in his local community, a place that once felt welcoming. Now, he sensed an unease in the air: individuals who would chat freely about Ukraine in generalities but never once turned to him, looked him in the eye, and said, "Maksym, how are you holding up?" That silence amplified his sense of loneliness. "It was like I was carrying this huge weight that nobody else wanted to even look at," Maksym said. "Just one person asking me how I was doing would have meant the world."

Maksym explained how many of his colleagues and community members probably didn't know how to start the conversation, or they feared saying the wrong thing. Some had little awareness or education about talking through painful war-related issues; others believed that bringing it up would only burden him more. Meanwhile, cultural norms at his workplace and in his community discouraged personal conversations, especially ones involving war or politics. The end result? Maksym felt invisible. His entire emotional world went unheard.

Hearing me talk about communities and companies that teach people how to engage in uncomfortable discussions rather than dodge them made Maksym wish he belonged to such a community himself. "We needed those skills in my workplace. I needed it in my community," he said. "Just to have people open up and ask, 'How are you really feeling?' That's all it would have taken."

I asked Maksym if he'd be open to sharing more about how he felt back then and how he feels now. He agreed, speaking with a frankness and clarity that took my breath away. He described anger, sorrow, betrayal, and hope. "Maybe this time, we'll talk about it. Maybe this time, we'll face it together," he said. Listening to him so openly name his pain and longing reminded me just how powerful genuine curiosity and compassion can be.

Maksym's story underscores the price we pay for avoiding difficult topics: isolation, hurt, and deeper disconnection. It shows how politeness or even "respectful silence" can ironically become a barrier that prevents people from truly hearing one another. When communities and workplaces don't teach and model the skills for these awkward, even messy conversations, those like Maksym are left feeling both unheard and alone.

I tell Maksym's story here to remind us that a deliberate, respectful question is a powerful tool we might all consider adding to our tool kit. We can learn when and how to risk speaking up with a single question, even something simple like "How are you holding up?" so we can break through silence and invite a moment of profound connection. It can mean the difference between someone feeling invisible or cared for.

A single question, "How are you holding up?" can break through silence and invite a moment of profound connection.

TECHNIQUES FOR BEING DELIBERATE

The art of questioning is about being deliberate, intentional, and consistent. It's about creating space for genuine curiosity and staying open to different outcomes, without demanding or pushing others into a defensive stance.

Being deliberate in questioning means slowing down, choosing your words carefully, and making room for both inquiry and response. It means establishing rituals that allow for consistent, intentional questioning. Building a practice that helps us grow, connect, and break down walls, one thoughtful question at a time.

Being deliberate with our questions isn't just about how we ask in the moment. It's also about who we invite into our questioning journey. When we surround ourselves with people who ask thoughtful questions and challenge our thinking with kindness, we develop our own capacity for curiosity and open-mindedness. This is why finding our own Frank can be so transformative for our growth and connection.

Timing Is Everything

When it comes to questioning, timing is everything. Slowing down lets us be deliberate and ask questions in a way that invites people in instead of pushing them away. It lets us create room for a genuine dialogue, not just an exchange of opinions.

Here's how slowing down can make all the difference:

- **Pause before speaking.** There's always a right time to pose a question and a right time to stop talking and listen instead. Pausing before going into action gives us space to consider not just what we will say, but how we will say it.

- **Breathe before responding.** Take several deep breaths, especially in tense moments. This simple practice can completely shift how you deliver your words, allowing you to choose the most appropriate tone, body language, and phrasing.

- **Embrace the silence.** Enjoy the pauses in conversations. Give everyone time to think. Remember the listening lesson I learned back in China where silence held a different meaning than I was used to? This was a test to see who could hold the silence longer, so silence was a sign of respect, a moment for reflection, not something to be hurried through or filled.

Rituals for Questioning

When I first moved to California, the culture shock was so great that I felt isolated. One of the tactics I used to build bridges was to reach out to people I admired on social media, whether a content creator, a writer, or poet to offer my support and friendship. Many took me up on that offer, and eventually these individuals and groups and I have ritualized our meetings by reserving the same day every month for gatherings.

As a result, I am now in a monthly women's group where we support each other with a focus on personal growth and having the best relationships we can have. I am also in three different entrepreneurial groups with monthly meetings: in Ukraine, China, and a global group of ten people, each from a different continent.

What I discovered from the evolution of these connections and friendships is that having a constant cadence creates safety and allows us to go deeper. That's why I consider creating rituals around questioning to be another important aspect of being deliberate.

Questioning shouldn't just happen in reactive moments; it can be something we practice proactively, as part of our daily lives. Creating rituals for inquiry helps set the stage correctly and then consistently builds habits of approaching others with curiosity and care.

For example, since I live with my parents, we encounter situations that call for questioning, such as how we take care of the kids or how we balance our cultural practices in our multicultural family. To manage these moments deliberately, we established a ritual: a monthly dinner, just my parents and me, where we connect, share, and talk about the kids in a calm, relaxed environment. This dedicated time makes a world of difference in how we approach these challenging discussions.

Another ritual involves my husband and me. We make a point of having a monthly meeting, just the two of us. During this meeting, we take turns asking each other these questions:

- What subjects are hard for you to talk about?
- What is your biggest fear right now?
- What do you care most about?
- How can I support you best?
- Is there anything I can do to make your life better?

One person speaks while the other just listens. This is our way of creating space to question and understand each other's needs more deeply. It's our ritual that keeps our partnership strong and healthy.

I have now shared this ritual numerous times in the workshops and coaching sessions that I lead. After each of these different settings, I always have participants follow up with me saying that they tried the ritual with their partner, children, or even business associates and they were impressed at how well it works to connect, uncover subjects that people usually don't dare to speak up about, and just get to know each other better. Because only one person speaks at a time, with no space for defensiveness or arguing, we are able to create a deeper understanding of what each person truly thinks and feels. Try this out, and let me know how it works for you!

These rituals build a muscle that makes questioning deliberate and effective, even when the moment is spontaneous. Like when Jerome "elevated out of conflict" while at the air pump at the gas station, his ability to pause, question his reaction, and choose a different approach benefited from all the practice he's had through our questioning rituals.

PAUSING WITH INTENTION

The art of questioning isn't about asking questions impulsively or firing them off like bullets. It's about slowing down and being intentional with every aspect of how we interact with another person or group: our timing, tone, and context. This deliberate approach allows us to choose our words carefully, pick the right moment, and create an environment where meaningful exchange is possible.

Importantly, slowing down isn't hesitating; it's pausing with intention. When we hesitate, we're often frozen by uncertainty or fear. But when we deliberately slow down, we're creating space for thoughtfulness. It's the difference between stumbling because you're unsure and pausing because you're being strategic.

Step 2

ASK THE INTERESTED QUESTION

	State	Step 1	Step 2	Step 3
PRINCIPLE 4 The Art of Questioning	From Defensive to Interested	Be Deliberate	Ask the Interested Question	Question Together

When someone asks you a question, how often do you have no desire to answer them? Was it the way they asked the question? Were they truly curious or were they simply looking for confirmation of their own opinion? And let's be honest: How often have you done the same to others?

Curiosity matters, especially when we're questioning traditions and norms, whether in our personal life, relationships, or company. It's easy to fall into the trap of wanting validation for our own beliefs instead of genuinely seeking to understand someone else's perspective. But if we want to challenge traditions effectively and invite others into that process, we have to ask curious, open-minded, and genuinely interested questions.

Being truly curious can open doors that we didn't even know were closed. It allows us to avoid defensiveness, making space for respectful dialogue that invites new information rather than just reinforcing what we think we know. Asking such questions earns us permission to explore further, leading to deeper responses, more meaningful conversations, and, quite often, unexpected breakthroughs.

To be clear, this isn't about softening our tone or being unclear on purpose. I am all for simple, direct, and clear language. I believe in speaking to others as two adults, trusting that the other person can handle the truth. I personally dislike it when people beat around the bush; I want to know what they really mean. As I mentioned in the opening to Principle 4, I am uncomfortable with blind spots and try to constantly question myself and my surroundings to make sure I understand what's happening. As such, I rely on other people to tell me what they think and see about me, especially in the places where it is harder to see myself.

There's a difference between being direct and asking leading questions or being sarcastic. I can be direct and curious at the same time. Being sarcastic or using disguised assertions makes it much harder to stay curious. Being direct while staying open and curious is how we earn trust and lead meaningful change.

Reassurance: You Won't Lose Real Relationships

One of the biggest fears I hear is: "If I start speaking up more, people will think I'm difficult or argumentative." I understand this fear because I've felt it too.

Here's what I've discovered: The people who truly care about you want to know what you're really thinking. They're relieved when you're authentic instead of pretending everything is fine. And the relationships that can't handle your honest, respectful voice? Those weren't serving you anyway.

When you learn to engage conflict with presence and curiosity, you don't become more difficult. You become more real. And my experience shows that real relationships are always stronger than polite ones.

THE POWER OF GENUINE CURIOSITY

Earlier, I shared how Tsering's "Indian head shake" taught me about cultural differences in nonverbal communication. Remember how I initially misinterpreted Tsering's side-to-side head movement as "no" when it often meant "yes"? There's more to that story, a moment that showed me how genuine curiosity goes beyond simply clarifying gestures to creating profound connection. While I had learned to recognize this cultural difference, I hadn't yet experienced the transformative power of truly curious questions until facing a parenting challenge.

My oldest son was in conflict with some classmates at school, and I was torn between different approaches: Should I teach him to stand up for himself or encourage him to report the situation to teachers? I desperately wanted Tsering's perspective, not just as my friend, but as someone who had navigated childhood conflicts across different cultural contexts.

When I asked for her advice, she gave her characteristic head tilt. This time, however, I didn't just want to correctly interpret her gesture, I wanted to deeply understand her thinking. Instead of asking a leading question like "So you don't think he should stand up to the bully?" I approached with genuine curiosity.

"I value your perspective on this," I said. "Could you share more about how children in your culture learn to handle conflict? What values guided your family's approach to these situations?"

The conversation that followed was remarkable. Tsering didn't just give me a quick answer; she shared stories from her childhood in India, explained Tibetan principles of compassionate strength, and offered nuanced perspectives I would never have considered.

"In my tradition," she explained, "we teach children that standing up for yourself doesn't have to mean aggression. There's a middle path between passivity and violence."

She described specific practices her parents had taught her, ways to maintain dignity without escalating conflict, phrases that disarmed aggression without submission, and the importance of community in addressing harmful behaviors.

This wasn't just about understanding a head movement anymore, it was about entering a whole new framework for thinking about conflict resolution. By asking questions from genuine curiosity rather than assumed understanding, I discovered an approach to bullying that incorporated wisdom from a tradition thousands of years old.

What had begun as a simple clarification of a nonverbal cue had evolved into something much deeper. My curious questions created space for Tsering to share not just her opinion but her cultural heritage. And it was this heritage, not just her personal advice, that ultimately helped my son navigate his situation with both courage and compassion.

Truly curious questions don't just solve misunderstandings, they open doors to worlds we might never otherwise enter. When we ask questions not just to confirm what we think we know but to discover what we don't even know we don't know, we truly learn.

Framing Curious Questions

Since I just shared a story about lessons I learned by asking curious questions in a cultural context, let me stick with that setting to show ways in which you can be curious without being confrontational.

EXAMPLE 1: "I'M CURIOUS ABOUT THIS TRADITION. HOW DID IT START?"

When my French in-laws insisted on certain holiday rituals, like serving both fish and meat during Passover, or reciting a prayer for the French Republic at the end of Shabbat evening service, I felt a quiet resistance. But instead of brushing them off, I asked where those customs came from.

That one question shifted everything.

I learned that the fish and meat symbolized abundance and postwar resilience, a way of reclaiming joy after loss. And the Republic prayer? It stretches back centuries. In the Talmud, a core principle, *Dina de-malkhuta dina*, "The law of the kingdom is the law," guided how Jews practiced their faith while living under other rulers. In France, the tradition of praying for the king dates back to the twelfth century, and was formalized by Napoleon in 1808. It became a prayer for the Republic and is still recited every Saturday in synagogues tied to the French Consistory (the official organization representing French Jewish communities since Napoleon's era).

Suddenly, what felt foreign became familiar. I wasn't just witnessing rituals, I was being invited into a story of continuity, dignity, and belonging. All it took was one small act of curiosity.

EXAMPLE 2: "PLEASE TELL ME MORE ABOUT THIS RULE AND THE REASONS BEHIND IT."

When joining a nonprofit board, I encountered a policy requiring a three-step approval process for all financial decisions. Instead of pushing to change what seemed bureaucratic, I asked the executive director to explain its purpose. Learning it had been implemented after a financial scandal years earlier helped me see its value as a safeguard, allowing us to refine rather than eliminate it.

EXAMPLE 3: "WHAT EXACTLY DOES FLEXIBILITY MEAN TO YOU IN THIS CONTEXT?"

During a tense negotiation with a Chinese manufacturing partner who kept insisting on "flexibility" in our agreement, I asked for specific examples of what flexibility meant to them. This clarified they were concerned about seasonal production challenges rather than trying to change pricing or quality standards, which led to a mutually beneficial compromise.

QUESTIONS TO AVOID: LEADING, DISGUISED ASSERTIONS, AND SARCASM

Not all questions foster growth and understanding. Some questions may seem curious on the surface but are loaded with bias or assumptions that only push people away. Here are the types of questions to avoid:

AVOID LEADING QUESTIONS

Leading questions and specific word choices try to subtly push the other person toward a particular answer that confirms our own biases.

"Wouldn't you agree that this is the only logical solution?" The use of *wouldn't* instead of *do you agree?* here seems to attempt to corner the person.

"Surely you think this is the best way to handle things, right?" Again, the use of *surely* seems to be a way to subtly pressure the person toward a certain answer.

There are specific types of questions that imply that there's only one acceptable answer, and those questions shut down open exploration. Instead, try asking genuinely open questions like, "What are your thoughts on how we could handle this?"

For example, at Les Lunes, during our early design discussions, we often used leading questions. I remember asking the team, "Don't you think this dress should be blue?" implying that blue was the only viable option. This closed off other ideas, stifling creativity and genuine input.

After our breakthrough involving customer input in the design process, we learned the importance of being open to a variety of perspectives. Instead of pushing my own ideas, I shifted to asking, "What color do you think would resonate most with our customers?"

This simple shift opened the space for genuine discussion and diverse input. I welcomed everyone's opinions and encouraged questions, not just about design, but about every aspect of the business.

By removing leading questions and focusing on open-ended, genuinely curious questions, our company culture began to change. We set a tone of openness, where questioning was encouraged and everyone felt heard. This helped us innovate more effectively and design products that truly met our customers' needs. The change wasn't just in what we created but how we created, and that led to a more collaborative environment where inventiveness thrived.

Disguised assertions are statements masquerading as questions. They do not invite dialogue but instead carry an underlying criticism or push an agenda.

"Why would you think that?" (meaning: "You think that and therefore, you're wrong.")

"Is it impossible for you to do it differently?" (meaning: "You are doing it wrong.")

"Do you have to do it this way?" (meaning: "You are doing it wrong.")

Instead of these disguised assertions, be direct but open. For example, "I'm curious about your reasoning for choosing this approach. Could you share more?"

Here are some examples for reference:

Conflict with a Friend About Social Engagements

Disguised Assertion: "Why do you always cancel our plans every time we commit to doing something together?"

The implication here is that the friend is unreliable or not committed. This disguised assertion creates defensiveness and closes off an honest conversation.

Alternative: "I noticed you've had to cancel our plans a few times lately. Is there something else going on that we could discuss?"

This alternative phrasing opens the door to understanding without judgment. It invites the friend to share what's really happening.

Negotiating with a Supplier for Ethical Materials

Disguised Assertion: "Why can't you meet our sustainability requirements? Isn't that what you agreed to?"

This disguised assertion implies that the supplier is falling short of their commitments and can easily make them defensive. It doesn't leave much room for dialogue or problem-solving.

Alternative: "We're facing some challenges with meeting our sustainability requirements. Can you help me understand what obstacles are making it difficult?"

The alternative phrasing invites a collaborative approach. It assumes that both parties want to meet the sustainability goals, and it opens up the conversation to explore the challenges together.

Addressing Concerns with a Business Partner

Disguised Assertion: "Is it impossible for you to stick to the schedule we agreed on?"

The disguised assertion here makes the other person feel blamed for not meeting expectations and shuts down productive dialogue.

Alternative: "I'd like to understand what's making it challenging to stay on schedule. Are there obstacles we can address together?"

AVOID SARCASTIC QUESTIONS

Sarcasm is the fastest way to create defensiveness and resentment. Sarcastic questions are usually veiled criticisms that generally sabotage the atmosphere needed for open dialogue. These usually cover up strong hidden feelings on the part of the questioner or contain requests intended to make the other person feel vulnerable.

"Do you always have to make things difficult?"

"Is it possible for you to focus for even a minute?"

Instead, try asking directly: "I'm having a hard time understanding this. How can we make it clearer?" or, "How can I support you to stay focused on this task?"

Along these lines, when I needed a show of affection, like a hug, it was hardest for me to ask for it when I most needed it: during those most vulnerable moments. Instead of simply asking for what I needed, I would say something sarcastic like, "Are you just going to stand there?"

Did this ever get me the hug I so wanted? Not once. It allowed me to keep my pride intact, but it didn't get me what I actually needed, which was human connection.

The first time I directly asked for a hug, the results "magically" appeared. I was hugged. I received exactly what I needed, and the other person was liberated from an uncomfortable situation. He didn't have to guess what I wanted; I made it clear. That directness deepened our relationship and opened up new ways for us to support each other. It made me realize how counterproductive sarcasm was. It created confusion instead of clarity, and distance instead of closeness.

Asking the right kind of questions, open, curious, and nonjudgmental, can break through defensiveness and lead to real growth. Let me share one more instance about how practicing the right type of questioning had a significant impact on my behavior and mindset.

QUESTION YOURSELF LIKE A FRIEND

I used to be very harsh on myself, always demanding perfection and punishing myself for even the smallest mistakes. Several friends started pointing this out to me. They noticed how I talked about myself and how unforgiving I was.

At first, I got defensive: "Everyone talks like this when they want to progress," or, "This is how I succeeded; why stop now?" I resisted their feedback.

But my friends didn't give up. They used gentle, open-ended questions to help me see what I couldn't see myself. They asked, "What would it feel like if you were gentler with yourself?" or, "What would happen if you treated yourself like you treat a friend?" These questions weren't accusations; they were invitations to reflect. They made me feel safe enough to consider another perspective.

Their questions allowed me to slowly recognize the impact of my self-talk. It made me curious: What if I could achieve my goals without being so harsh? What if I could be kind to myself?

I started experimenting with using the names my parents and older brother called me as a child. "Annushka," "Anechka," "Annyuta." Addressing myself this way worked like magic, bringing kindness and compassion into my self-talk. Every night as I wrote in my diary, I found I could forgive myself for mistakes. This simple practice made me more willing to take risks and make new mistakes the next day.

And you know what? It didn't make me weaker. It made me more resilient, more open to growth.

This shift showed me the true power of questioning. When questions are genuine and free of judgment, they can break through even the most ingrained defenses. They invite us to reconsider, to reflect, and ultimately, to grow.

GENUINE CURIOSITY CHANGES RELATIONSHIPS

Curiosity breaks down walls. Asking real, open questions isn't just a skill; it changes relationships, solves conflicts, and leads to deeper understanding.

Whether we're questioning a cultural norm, asking for support, or trying something new, curiosity makes all the difference. It cuts through defensiveness, sparks real conversations, and builds true connection and growth.

If you want meaningful conversations, skip the sarcasm and leading questions. Be genuinely interested. When people feel safe, when they aren't being judged or backed into a corner, they open up. Growth happens when it's invited, not forced.

I learned to be kinder to myself because my friends asked me the right questions. They challenged my harsh self-talk without judgment. This is true for all of us whether we're leading a team, supporting family, or just trying to be better to ourselves. The right questions can open doors, invite reflection, and create real change.

The art of asking interested questions transforms not just our one-on-one interactions but also how we navigate different cultures, communities, and the broader world. As we develop this skill, we discover that questioning can become a collective practice, a way of exploring together that helps us understand the sources of potential conflict, and it creates understanding far beyond what any of us could achieve alone.

Step *3*

QUESTION TOGETHER

	State	Step 1	Step 2	Step 3
PRINCIPLE 4 The Art of Questioning	From Defensive to Interested	Be Deliberate	Ask the Interested Queston	Question Together

Three times in my life I have moved to a different country; each has had a culture very different from my Ukrainian roots. And each move led me to questioning fundamental parts of myself, such as my identity, professional approaches, and lifestyle choices. Doing it alone was overwhelming, and I dealt with internal doubts and external misunderstandings.

But then I remembered a lesson I'd learned long ago: I didn't have to navigate this journey in isolation. Making connections with others as we question together has led to a life where I am rewarded with ongoing valuable insights and connection.

ADOPTING A NEW CULTURE

My way of understanding a country and retaining my identity at the same time became what I call "adopting the country." This is how I learned to question together with an entire culture.

In 1993, when I turned seventeen, it was time for me to choose the path of my future studies. But instead, I felt a strong urge to leave my home, travel to other countries, and discover the world. I longed to meet people who were different from me and to learn and connect with them. However, it seemed impossible for me to do what so many other young people around the world did routinely. The Soviet Union had collapsed a couple of years earlier, and the borders were as good as closed since it was impossible to get visas to travel to most countries. I started applying everywhere for scholarships, visas, and any programs and opportunities to get out. I failed and failed.

Then I heard about a program established by the Chinese government in several Ukrainian universities in which students could study Mandarin and Chinese Studies. For those students who could master the Mandarin language well enough to enter a Chinese university, China would provide scholarships and visas.

"What a great idea!" I thought. "I could learn a new language and about this unique culture, and I might even have an opportunity to go and discover China!" I was already imagining leaving my parents' home and traveling alone to uncharted lands, having adventures I only read about in books and meeting all kinds of people different from me. I dreamed of travels, explorations, and new learnings.

I rushed to the admissions office, and to my surprise, I found no line! It turned out that very few students ever applied for this program, while the lines for learning Western languages (English, French, German) were very long. My family and friends were not supportive to say the least;

many were shocked and a few even made fun of my plan. "What do you know about China? They are poor, uneducated savages who only eat rice . . ." You can insert whatever stereotypes you may have about any other random country or people. I said, "You're right. I don't know anything about China, and neither do you. But I am interested in going and finding out everything I don't know!"

This response became my first practice in questioning together, not just accepting what others assumed to be true, but inviting them into genuine curiosity.

I applied and was accepted into the program. I loved being part of it! I was so proud to be one of very few students studying Chinese in my city called Dnipropetrovsk (now Dnipro). I would take a Chinese textbook and ride on public transportation for hours proudly showing off my book and catching surprised stares from others. I pasted Post-its with Chinese characters all over the house and dreamed of giant characters floating all around me in my sleep. Throwing myself fully at the language, I was quickly fluent.

It seemed that before I knew it, I was on the plane going to study at Sichuan University, in Chengdu City, Sichuan Province, China. I applied myself fully in my classes, and spent all my free time with the locals, discovering the country and the people. Every chance I got to take some time off, I traveled alone with a little backpack through China and Tibet, exploring, discovering, and learning.

I was fascinated by the fact that besides the Han Chinese majority, there are fifty-five other ethnic minority groups living in China, totaling about 105 million people. I took every opportunity to visit these ethnic minority groups, and questioning became a pathway to deeper understanding of both their cultures and my own. Growing up as an ethnic minority myself, I initially wanted to connect and see how these groups lived and thrived in the country where 92% of the population is Han. I wanted to understand what gave them the strength and desire to persevere and maintain their own culture. Every group had a different language, music, food, traditions. I managed to stay curious and learned all I could.

The Choice to Adopt Rather Than Adapt

Somewhere in those early months, I faced a fundamental choice. I could approach China as an outsider trying to adapt, learning enough to get by, staying polite but distant, maintaining the comfortable assumption that this was temporary. Or I could do something much more vulnerable: I could adopt China as part of who I am.

I became clearer and clearer about the difference between adapting and adopting through the questions I was willing to ask. When you're adapting, you ask practical questions: How do I navigate this system? What are the rules I need to follow? When you're adopting, you ask transformational questions: How does this way of thinking expand who I can become? What do these values teach me about life that I wouldn't learn otherwise?

I chose to adopt.

This meant learning Mandarin so fluently that people couldn't tell on the phone that I wasn't Chinese. It meant spending hours learning to play mah-jongg until I was invited to wedding tables as part of the community. I once attended a wedding in Chengdu City where I was surprised to find the courtyard packed with rows of square and rectangular tables. Each table was a hub of excitement, surrounded by guests deeply engrossed in the game. Hearing the rhythmic clatter of mah-jongg tiles blended with the conversations all around and seeing the newlyweds having to compete for attention against the excitement of the raucous games was an unforgettable experience. I even ended up being invited to one of the tables to play, accepted swiftly, as one of the community due to my language, and, more importantly, my mah-jongg skills.

Adopting China meant trying century eggs, a Chinese delicacy that are visually striking with their dark, translucent, amber-like whites and creamy, deep-greenish-black yolks. The complex flavors of earthiness and sharpness, and a pungent, savory aroma were characteristic of life in China, and I grew to love them. And then there was stinky tofu, a fermented tofu that has a strong odor (it is often fermented for months), which became my go-to snack during trips around the countryside. I wasn't trying these as a curious tourist sampling exotic foods, but as someone genuinely embracing the cultural experience of taste and tradition.

People who know me well say I transform when I speak Chinese. It's not that I turn into someone else; it's more that I adopted China so fully that it opened a part of me that would have otherwise stayed hidden. That part of me that simply connected and stayed connected with the country and its people in a profoundly deep way.

QUESTIONING ACROSS DIVIDES: LEARNING FROM FIFTY-SIX COMMUNITIES

I have always been fascinated by cultures that maintain their identity while living as minorities in larger societies. At seventeen, studying in Sichuan University in Chengdu, I discovered that China is home to fifty-six different ethnic groups. I became obsessed with a question that was really about my own life: Can we keep our cultural roots while thriving in a culture different from ours?

With my small backpack and walking shoes, I set out to visit as many of these communities as possible. But what I discovered wasn't just academic knowledge about different cultures. It became a practice of questioning together about the biggest challenges of identity and belonging.

Every group had different languages, music, food, traditions. But the questions we explored together were remarkably similar:

How do you pass your culture to the next generation when the world around you is changing?

How do you decide which traditions to keep and which to adapt?

How do you create belonging in a world that often sees you as different?

I took a twenty-six-hour train to visit the Li people in southern China, where I was welcomed into their boat-shaped homes. Community living was central to their society, and I was captivated by their collective approach to life. But what I noticed wasn't just their traditions. It was how they questioned me right back.

"How do you stay connected to your people when you're so far away?" one elder asked. "What keeps your culture alive in your heart when you're surrounded by different ways?" These questions got me thinking because I was struggling with exactly these issues.

During my month walking through Tibet, I was invited by monks at the Sakya Monastery to witness something few outsiders see: their practice of debating religious texts. I sat for hours watching monks in red and yellow robes taking turns to argue, listening to the hypnotic sounds of chanting. But beyond witnessing their practice, I found myself in conversations about different ways of seeking truth.

"How do you question your beliefs without losing your faith?" I asked them. Their responses and their questions back to me about my own spiritual journey became a form of questioning together that shaped how I approach uncertainty even today.

Through these experiences, I learned that questioning together across differences isn't about finding the same answers. It's about discovering that we're all struggling with similar human challenges, just from different starting points. Each community became a thinking partner in figuring out how to navigate the tension between staying true to who you are and adapting to the world around you.

This practice of questioning together, especially with people who see the world differently, is how I've survived and thrived through three immigrations while keeping my roots. The more we question together across our differences, the more we discover what we actually share beneath our conflicts.

> *The more we question together across our differences, the more*
> *we discover what we actually share beneath our conflicts.*

LESSONS FROM QUESTIONING TOGETHER

The greatest lesson I learned from my curious adventures was an inwardly focused one. Our tendency to judge others is directly related to our self-confidence and self-worth. **Noticing what we judge about others repeatedly can reveal what we do not accept about ourselves.** But ceasing to pass judgment on others leads to more self-love and acceptance, resulting in better personal and professional well-being.

Once I recognized this, my perspective on the world changed fundamentally. No longer did I see groups of people fighting over a limited slice of the pie. I saw people of all cultures and classes coming together to exponentially expand the size of the pie. And as a result of this connection to China, I ultimately became an expert in Chinese society and business, and was able to build two successful global companies. In case you are thinking, "Wow that's impressive!" it really wasn't. I was desperate. I had to build a life for myself and find a way to success and to realizing my dreams. Because the Chinese way of thinking and being opened up my perspectives and became a big part of my identity, I was able to translate those qualities into the making of my businesses.

And through my adventures, I gained incredible perspective into the complexity of the culture I was living in. My own curiosity and what I learned about suspending judgments brought me the opportunity to be seen as one of the community, and as such, I was able to experience trust, collaboration, learning, and finally, business success, in a country far from my original comfort zone.

QUESTIONING TOGETHER IN THE WORKPLACE

This practice of questioning together across differences isn't just something I discovered traveling through China. It's something I've taught in workshops and private sessions around the world.

In Beijing, I worked with a team of Chinese and American executives who were struggling to collaborate. The Americans thought the Chinese were being indirect and evasive. The Chinese thought the Americans were being rude and impatient. Both sides were frustrated and starting to avoid working together.

During our session, instead of trying to solve their communication problems, I asked them to get curious about their different approaches. What did directness mean in American culture? What did harmony mean in Chinese culture? How had their childhood experiences shaped their professional expectations?

By the end of that workshop, the American executives understood that what they'd interpreted as evasion was actually careful consideration of group dynamics. The Chinese executives realized that what they'd seen as rudeness was actually an American way of showing respect through directness.

A year later, I heard from their team leader. They had just completed their most successful product launch in company history. He mentioned that he believes the breakthrough didn't come from eliminating their cultural differences, but from learning to see those differences as strengths rather than obstacles.

LEARNING TO QUESTION TOGETHER

The many cultural experiences I've had, including living and building businesses in three different countries that were not my place of origin, have honed several important skills and stretched certain muscles in me, and I am grateful for these experiences. I've found the following three skills to be essential in creating conditions where questioning together can occur:

- Be curious and open-minded
- Be brave
- Seek to form meaningful friendships

Be Curious

While in China, I heard many visiting foreigners frequently complain about Chinese people spitting directly onto the floor. "They don't cover their mouth; it is as if they have no shame!" This action was seen as especially bad in restaurants and was the most distressing complaint I heard. It was followed by a sense of disgust and the assumption that what was happening was not okay and needed to stop.

I get it. The first time I experienced this behavior, I was not prepared for it and did not understand it either. This is what happened.

I was dining in a restaurant for a business lunch that was a very typical local eatery in Chengdu, the capital of Sichuan Province in Southwestern China. It was small and bustling with people, a modest place with plastic tables and stools packed tightly together. The air was filled with the aroma of sizzling stir-fry mingled with the scent of hot spices. The floor was a mosaic of faded tiles, visibly worn from the years of foot traffic and stains. At my table, fragrant dishes started arriving one by one, including my favorite, mapo tofu, spicy and numbing with Sichuan peppercorns.

I was excited about indulging in all the tantalizing food, but just as I reached for my chopsticks, my business date leaned back, cleared his throat with a deep, resonant sound, and then seemed to gather the contents of his throat into his mouth, which he then unceremoniously spat onto the tiled floor beside him. I was stunned and stared in shock at the floor, coming face to face with multiple small puddles of questionable origin on the once deep terracotta surface.

The sound of the prolonged clearing of his throat and the satisfaction he seemed to derive from the process moved me from an initial wave of revulsion to curiosity. What was this about? I sensed there was something I was missing. So, I did what a child might do in a strange situation. I was brutally honest, and I asked him about it, right to his face.

"Don't you do the same?" he asked. "What else do you do after you clear your throat from things that should not be there? Surely you do not just swallow all that stuff! It is very bad for your health, and needs to come out of your body!"

That's when I got my first lesson about the relationship Chinese people have with their bodies, their health, their food, and medicine. Traditional Chinese medicine is deeply rooted in ancient Chinese philosophy; it focuses on balance and harmony within the body. Examinations include looking at the tongue, checking the pulse, and assessing the emotional state of the person to find possible imbalances in the body's energy. Food is seen as medicine, and doctors prescribe specialized diets to restore balance and initiate self-healing. There is an emphasis on preventive healthcare and maintaining a well-rounded state of wellness in the mind, body, and spirit, and these principles are reflected in everyday culture and lifestyle. So instead of looking at behaviors I saw as unacceptable because they differed from my own social and cultural norms, I started asking for the reasons and stories behind these behaviors.

This experience shows why the first skill is to stay *curious and open-minded* no matter what, despite the fact that we might be surprised, shocked, appalled, or scared, since being exposed to the unknown and unfamiliar will make us feel any number of uncomfortable sensations. Yet it is vital to keep demanding: "Tell me more!"

Be Brave

Amy Chua wrote: "Do you know what a foreign accent is? It's a sign of bravery." It is scary to leave the known behind, even when the known is not comfortable or safe. We are all wary of the unknown. It is also very uncomfortable to be different in a new environment, to stand out as someone who is foreign, who does not follow the social rules and norms and who might even look different.

I feel this sense of being different very acutely in France. In fact, every time I order food in a restaurant or bread at the boulangerie, I call on my bravest self to ask in French for what I want. Have you tried it, and do you know that look on the face of a French waiter when a foreigner tries to speak French? At first, I judged French people as language snobs or even perceived their lack of willingness to understand a non-native

French accent as dislike of foreigners. But after asking any number of times "Why?" I now understand there are many more layers in why the French seemingly behave in a certain way.

French people *love* their language. There is a deep-rooted cultural emphasis on the French language's integrity and a strong desire to preserve its unique characteristics. French people study it deeply and diligently and will correct each other (without fear or regret) when someone uses bad grammar.

Once I learned this about the French, I became more open to the corrections and suggestions of the native French speakers. But I still need to gather all my courage to order that amazing *pain au chocolat* at the boulangerie next door...

Form Meaningful Friendships

The third muscle that I continue to stretch as an immigrant is the ability to form new meaningful friendships. I think about this as reestablishing a large family in every place I move to; as building that village that is so necessary for us to learn, thrive, raise kids, support and be supported, and to find that sense of belonging.

Establishing meaningful friendships leads not only to better, more fulfilling new lives, it also offers the chance for a more profound understanding of the local community, its culture, and traditions. Friendships bring social engagement into the immigrants' lives, providing for their emotional support and understanding as they struggle to adapt to the new cultural environment.

How do we form new meaningful friendships, especially later on in life? Of course, each person's journey is unique, and what works for one individual may not be the same for another. What does unite us is that we all face the same challenges and have the same resources: It takes time, patience, effective communication, empathy, self-confidence, shared interests, and curiosity. And it certainly requires stepping out of one's comfort zone, over and over again.

I was fortunate to enter into an extended family in China with my business partner George Hong at the head, who became like an older brother to me. George taught me to truly listen. I was not only accepted but very nearly adopted by his family. They invited me to important family celebrations, I visited his elderly parents in the hospital when they were sick, and I knew where their ancestors' ashes were kept. The memories we created together and the lessons I learned about China allowed me to know this country and its people deeply and intimately.

I also formed strong bonds with my dear Chinese sister Tracy Wang who was always there for me no matter what, and my other dear sisters in business Xiao Xiao and Ye Huan, whose business acumen and generosity are my inspirations forever. These three Chinese women opened the door into the reality of what a Chinese businesswoman is: someone who is strong and independent who defies the old traditions of society while carrying deep knowledge and respect for its culture. I was surrounded, supported, and nurtured by these friendships, and they gave me the sense of belonging over the twenty years I lived and built businesses in China. That I felt seen, understood, and accepted as a full member of the community was an invaluable consequence of seeking meaningful friendships.

THE LIBERATION OF QUESTIONING

We've explored how to transform questions from defensive reactions to invitations that open doors: slow down and establish rituals, ask questions that break down walls, and expand from individual practice to collective questioning that bridges cultures.

Frank challenges me to sharpen my thinking while maintaining our connection. My journeys through China opened doors to understanding cultures vastly different from my own. Patient questioning helped me find belonging in new countries and build bridges across seemingly uncrossable divides. Each experience confirms that questions, when asked with genuine curiosity and care, have an extraordinary power to transform relationships.

These three elements of questioning work as an integrated practice. Deliberate questioning creates the intentional space where genuine interest can flourish. Interested questions build the trust that makes collective questioning possible. And questioning together expands our understanding beyond what any individual perspective could achieve. When all three come together, even the most challenging differences and deep conflicts can transform into opportunities for connection.

What liberates us in the art of questioning is freedom from the burden of knowing everything. There's a lightness in genuine curiosity, a willingness to be surprised, to learn, to grow. Questions open doors that certainty keeps firmly shut.

As we move toward our final principle, The Rule of Us, I invite you to bring this spirit of questioning into your daily interactions. Where might you be more deliberate in how you ask? What questions could you frame with more genuine interest? Who could you invite into your questioning journey?

The practice of artful questioning prepares us for the ultimate shift in perspective: from seeing the world through the lens of "us versus them" to recognizing our fundamental connectedness. This recognition of our shared humanity, which we'll explore in Principle 5, allows us to truly live, love, and work together across our differences.

Our journey through the first four principles, engaging with presence, assuming nothing, listening to understand, and questioning with curiosity, has prepared us for this final and perhaps most transformative principle: the rule of us. By practicing these principles, we create the conditions for recognizing our fundamental connection as human beings, even across our deepest differences.

ASK FROM CURIOSITY, NOT CERTAINTY

The questions we ask reveal what we're ready to discover. I learned this during my discreet rebellion with Les Lunes, when questioning "Why must fashion be created this way?" opened pathways that challenging statements never could. Similarly, when my friend Frank challenged my business ideas, his persistent questions rather than quick judgments helped me develop stronger concepts. Our deepest collaborations often begin when we ask questions to understand rather than to confirm what we already believe.

Practice asking questions that connect through three approaches: First, catch yourself when you're about to make a quick assessment. Instead of dismissing an idea, approach it with thoughtful questioning that digs deeper than surface reactions. Next, craft questions that open doors rather than close them. Avoid disguised assertions like, "Why do you always cancel our plans?" and instead ask, "I noticed you've had to cancel plans a few times, is there something going on we could discuss?" Finally, ask with warmth, replacing sarcasm with directness, leading questions with genuine inquiry, and creating space with questions that invite the other person to share more fully.

Take a moment to record five genuine questions you could ask someone you find difficult to understand. Focus on questions that invite deeper reflection rather than defensiveness. Next time you're with this person, try introducing just one of these questions into your conversation. Pay attention not just to their verbal response but to their body language and energy. Notice how different it feels to approach them with questions born from genuine interest rather than judgment. Questions aren't just tools for gathering information. They're invitations to collaboration that can transform relationships when offered with sincerity and received with presence.

Reassurance: You Don't Need to Master Everything at Once

If Principle 4 feels more complex than the earlier principles, that's because it is. You're seeing how everything works together now, not just one skill at a time. That can feel overwhelming.

Here's what I want you to know. You don't need to integrate all four principles perfectly before you see results. I've watched people transform their most difficult relationships by consistently using just *one* principle well.

Maybe you're naturally good at questioning your assumptions but struggle with listening fully. Or you can stay present beautifully but still react defensively to certain triggers. That's completely normal.

The goal isn't to become expert at all of this before trying it. The goal is to notice which principle helps you most in which situations, then practice that one until it becomes natural. The integration happens on its own over time.

You're further along than you think.

THE RULE OF US

*	State	Step 1	Step 2	Step 3
PRINCIPLE 5 **The Rule** **of Us**	From Divided to Connected	Pop the Bubble	Let's Play	It's Okay to Share

Moving from Divided to Connected

Have you ever experienced a moment when something you held dear, your identity, your beliefs, your sense of belonging, suddenly seemed to fracture? I have. . . .

On February 24, 2022, my life as I knew it ended.

War broke out in my country of origin, Ukraine. Russia attacked Ukraine, killing, bombing, and destroying my homeland and my people. I felt personally attacked. Despite my life being about leaving my roots behind and embracing the ways of other cultures, this war struck a deep chord in my love for my country and my people. Adding to my pain was the reality that, while most Western countries rallied around Ukraine with aid and sanctions, China, my China, a country I deeply love and respect, aligned itself with Russia, the aggressor. It felt like a betrayal.

And Russia? It was the culture I grew up in and the language that remains my mother tongue. Speaking Russian, both within and outside the Ukrainian community, became an internal and external conflict for me. How could I continue speaking the language of the aggressor while witnessing atrocities committed by Russian soldiers?

We grew up speaking Russian, as Russification during the Soviet Union mandated. Policies of the time suppressed the use of Ukrainian, elevating Russian as the dominant language in schools, public institutions, and media. We learned to love the language: its songs, literature, and customs. But as the war unfolded, this love turned to turmoil.

I threw myself into anti-war efforts. For months, my life revolved around helping Ukraine, supporting refugees fleeing the country, assisting those who stayed behind to fight, helping Ukrainian entrepreneurs keep their businesses running, ensuring that salaries could be paid and infrastructure sustained, even in the face of devastation.

By night, I scrolled through horrifying images of the war, checked casualty statistics, and spoke to family and friends in Ukraine, praying they were still alive.

This experience revealed perhaps the most profound principle in our dance of conflict and connection. While the previous principles may help us cross the distance between individuals, this final principle, The Rule of Us, invites us to dissolve the very notion of separation itself. It's about moving beyond "you and me" to discover what becomes possible when we embrace "us."

That notion is what kept me going during these dark days. The Rule of Us involves finding common humanity, shifting the mindset from "I" and "you" to "us." It is about building bridges instead of deepening divides, even when emotions run high and differences seem insurmountable. How do we practice this when our homeland is at war?

ENGAGING IN US

One of the ways I've managed to keep moving forward was to engage with others who also believed in the rule of us. Here are three examples.

EnsembleUkraine: A Community of Action

My husband cofounded EnsembleUkraine, a group of French tech entrepreneurs working tirelessly to support Ukraine. Their efforts in those early, critical months saved lives.

EnsembleUkraine focused on microprojects, selecting initiatives with care and rigor to ensure they delivered real impact. What made EnsembleUkraine special was that initially, almost all volunteers were French people touched by the situation in Ukraine. They weren't helping "their own country." They were genuinely helping others. Later, as more Ukrainians fled the war, they joined the effort, finding purpose, hope, and connection through contributing.

Watching my husband rise an hour earlier each day and dedicate weekends and holidays to this cause inspired me deeply. It wasn't just about the money raised; it was about the spirit of collective action that brought people together across borders for a shared purpose.

Entrepreneurs' Organization:
A Global Network Uniting for Ukraine

My professional organization, Entrepreneurs' Organization (EO), also mobilized quickly. EO Poland took the lead, coordinating aid for Ukrainian refugees arriving in Europe and supporting Ukrainian entrepreneurs working to keep their businesses afloat.

This collective initiative highlighted the power of finding "us" amid crisis. Entrepreneurs from different countries, cultures, and political beliefs came together to make a tangible difference.

Global Solidarity: A Source of Strength

Every time I shared that I was originally from Ukraine, I was met with words of encouragement and stories of support. Whether in the US, France, or elsewhere, people cared about Ukraine's survival and wanted to help.

These examples of global solidarity continually remind me of humanity's interconnectedness. In moments of crisis, people often rise to help strangers, bound by shared values of compassion and justice.

THE HARDEST BRIDGE TO BUILD

The most challenging aspect of this time for me was connecting with the Russian community in France:

- My Russian neighbors who immigrated to France from Moscow many years ago and were instrumental and vital in my family's adaptation to the local community during our move to France

- My Russian friend with whom I went running and to yoga classes weekly

- My Russian lawyer, doctor, business partner, dance teacher, my kids' piano teacher, parents of my kids' friends at the local school

I was having trouble connecting with them all. I was angry. Suspicious of their intentions. How could I trust their sincerity in helping Ukraine while their government committed atrocities? I questioned how their actions, or inactions, might have contributed to Russia's aggression.

But the rule of us demanded that I face these feelings head-on.

As I navigated these intense emotions, I drew on the emotional mastery we explored in Step 1.2, recognizing how my anger was illuminating my values and using that understanding to choose my responses rather than being driven by reaction. The awareness practices from Step 3.1 helped me notice my emotions without being overwhelmed by them. This wasn't about suppressing legitimate feelings but about channeling them into connection rather than division.

Through this process, I began to see the humanity of these people around me. I asked them questions, and listened to their stories, witnessed their tears. Many were grappling with guilt and fear, deeply pained by their government's actions but unsure how to help.

And the deeper our connections, the more our trust grew.

This shift allowed us to work together toward a common goal: stopping the war and helping both Ukrainians and Russians build a better future. Many of my Russian friends and connections in France joined or even spearheaded the efforts of helping Ukrainian refugees, finding or giving them jobs, accommodation, and moral and financial support. All these efforts helped thousands of people, and the help still keeps coming.

In this journey, I rediscovered my love for the Russian language and culture, not as a weapon of war, but as a bridge that connects us. By embracing the shared humanity between Ukrainians, Russians, and others, I found a path forward that felt both authentic and hopeful.

FINDING COMMON HUMANITY AND MOVING FROM "I AND YOU" TO US

This principle builds on everything we've explored so far. The presence we cultivated in Principle 1 allows us to stay grounded even when differences threaten to pull us apart. The practice of assuming nothing from Principle 2 helps us see beyond the categories and labels that divide us. The deep listening we practiced in Principle 3 helps us to hear the humanity in others' experiences. And the art of questioning from Principle 4 helps us explore beyond the boundaries of our separate realities. All of these create the foundation for this final step: recognizing that despite our differences, we can fundamentally **collaborate**.

In the following chapters, we'll walk through the three steps that allow the change in focus from "I" to "we":

*	State	Step 1	Step 2	Step 3
PRINCIPLE 5 **The Rule of Us**	From Divided to Connected	Pop the Bubble	Let's Play	It's Okay to Share

- **Step 1: Pop the bubble.** Learn to pop the bubbles we surround ourselves with, breaking out of the information environments that keep us isolated in our perspectives.

- **Step 2: Let's play.** Discover how shared activities and play can create collaboration beyond words and make it easier to see through the shadows of conflict.

- **Step 3: It's okay to share.** It's easier for others to be open to you if you are open to others. It's okay to share ourselves authentically, creating spaces where others feel safe to do the same.

Step 1

POP THE BUBBLE

	State	Step 1	Step 2	Step 3
PRINCIPLE 5 The Rule of Us	From Divided to Connected	**Pop the Bubble**	Let's Play	It's Okay to Share

In 2022, I had a disturbing realization about how deeply my social media algorithms had affected my perspective on world events. I was having dinner with a colleague from a different political background, and we began discussing a recent news story. As we talked, it became clear we were literally living in different information universes. The story she described, the facts, the context, the implications, bore almost no resemblance to the version I had seen. Neither of us was making things up; we were simply repeating what our respective news sources had told us.

Curious and a bit unsettled, we pulled out our phones and compared our social media feeds side by side. The contrast was shocking. My feed was filled with articles, opinions, and perspectives that reinforced my existing worldview, while hers did the same for her beliefs. We were both intelligent, thoughtful people who believed we were well-informed, yet we had been existing in entirely separate information ecosystems.

That night changed how I consume information. I began deliberately seeking out perspectives different from my own, not to change my core values, but to understand the full context of issues and the legitimate concerns of people with different viewpoints. I started following thoughtful voices across the political spectrum, subscribing to newsletters that challenged my assumptions, and even attending events where I knew I'd be in the ideological minority.

This practice hasn't always been comfortable. I've had to confront my own biases and sometimes acknowledge valid points in arguments I instinctively wanted to dismiss. But it has made me more empathetic, more nuanced in my thinking, and ultimately more effective at building bridges with people different from myself.

The biggest surprise? Some of my own positions have evolved, not because I abandoned my values, but because I gained a more complete picture of complex issues. Popping my information bubble didn't make me less committed to my core principles. It made me more thoughtful about how to apply them in a world where most challenges don't have simple solutions.

How do we pop the information bubble that insulates us from others?

WHY BUBBLES EXIST

Why do we prefer to stay in our bubbles of information?

This is a crucial question, isn't it? Understanding why people prefer to stay in their bubbles of information and surround themselves with like-minded individuals is crucial for grasping the challenges we face in fostering connection and understanding in our divided world.

Psychologists and researchers have explored why this happens, and what they've found suggests several forces at play:

- **The comfort of confirmation bias.** We naturally look for information that confirms what we already believe and dismiss what contradicts us. It makes us feel certain and secure.

- **The allure of echo chambers.** Social media shows us more of what we already agree with. Before we know it, we're surrounded by people who think exactly like us. We start believing our views are more common than they actually are.

- **The need for emotional safety.** Connecting with people who see things differently can be exhausting, even threatening. It's easier to stay with people who share our values.

- **Social identity and group dynamics.** We get our sense of pride from the groups we belong to. Challenging our group's views feels like betrayal. Have you felt that pressure to conform? I have. So we stay in our bubbles where everyone agrees.

- **Fear of change and uncertainty.** Change is uncomfortable. When something challenges what we believe, we have to question everything. Most of us would rather stick with what feels stable and familiar.

We all carry biases. Not because we're bad people, but because we're human. The brain is wired for shortcuts, for confirming what we already believe and filtering out what challenges us. It's efficient, but it can also be dangerous. When we surround ourselves with people who think like us, we stop seeing the full picture. We build echo chambers that feel safe but limit our growth.

That's why stepping outside our comfort zone matters, not to agree with everything we hear, but to understand where others are coming from.

POPPING OUR BUBBLES

The most difficult step, I've discovered, is recognizing that it's part of our human nature to create bubbles of information around us that confirm our point of view and make us comfortable with only that information. Our bubble includes the actual information we consume due to the algorithms embodied in our searches and our social media profiles. Simply put, we humans prefer to surround ourselves with people who agree with us.

The second most difficult step is acknowledging and understanding that other people live in their bubble as well. This means that when we are exposed to people we may find ourselves in conflict with, we can be sure we do not know anything about what articles or TV programs they are exposed to, which books and movies they enjoy, or what conversations they have with their friends and families. What we *do* know is that most probably all these are different from what we are exposed to.

So basically, and in many ways, fundamentally, we do not live in the same world or operate with the same premises or principles.

Which raises the question: How can we even expect to connect with someone who comes from a different world without first learning about that world? I've learned it takes conscious effort on my part to break down established and constantly reinforced barriers, step by step.

One way to do that is to invoke Principle 4, The Art of Questioning, something we've come back to throughout this book. It's a powerful tool, one that allows us to step outside our habitual reactions and instead respond with curiosity and openness. By questioning our biases and genuinely listening to others, we make real connection possible.

Other examples of the process of popping the bubble include:

- Actively escaping your bubble with the help of technology (changing filters, using specialized apps) to expose yourself to other points of view

- Subscribing to other news channels and media that reflect opposing beliefs (from different political parties, different religions, different cultures)

- Seeking out books and movies promoted in the "opposing view" media

- Making friends in groups that you see as "others" and staying curious while spending time with them

These kinds of actions, changing filters and using specialized apps, subscribing to media that reflects opposing beliefs, seeking out books and movies cherished by people with different viewpoints, let us see the other side as more than a distant "them." They challenge us to engage with truths that might be uncomfortable, making room for a broader understanding.

These actions also help break down the narrative that paints others as inherently wrong. When we engage emotionally with their stories, it deepens empathy and reminds us that beneath political and ideological differences, we share similar experiences and emotions.

I experienced this firsthand during Russia's invasion in Ukraine. As painful as it was, I forced myself to read news sources from multiple perspectives: Ukrainian, Western, and yes, even Russian. While I strongly disagreed with Russian state media, understanding what Russians were being told helped me grasp why some Russians I knew held certain views. This didn't excuse the Russian invasion into Ukraine, but it gave me context that made conversation possible rather than impossible.

Another key action is to spend time with those we see as different from us. That makes what at first seems abstract into something more real and personal. We move from generalization and judgment to genuine curiosity and understanding. This awakening has the potential of transforming potential adversaries into real, complex individuals that we actually know, understand, and might even like and trust.

Escaping our bubble is not just about gaining new information, even though that is vital. It is also about challenging ourselves to understand the world from a different vantage point. The more we expose ourselves to other perspectives, the more we begin to challenge our own assumptions. When we challenge our assumptions, we are driven to understand why we believe as we believe.

Five Steps to Get You Started

Back in Chapter 1, I talked about Hope, a group of entrepreneurs who meet regularly to share perspectives and information about the crisis in the Middle East. The experience of that group reveals both the challenge and the possibility of connecting across different realities. While the psychology of confirmation bias and social identity makes it comfortable to remain in our bubbles, our monthly meetings prove that something powerful happens when we deliberately step outside them.

If you're inspired to step outside your own information bubble, here are some practical steps to consider:

- **Start small.** Choose one topic where you hold strong views and seek out a thoughtful perspective from "the other side." Don't begin with the most divisive issues.

- **Create a regular practice.** Like our monthly meetings, consistency helps build the mental muscles needed for this work.

- **Lead with feelings, not facts.** As we discovered in our meetings, sharing fears and hopes creates connection more effectively than debating information.

- **Find a conversation partner who shares your goal of understanding.** This work is easier when both people are committed to the process.

- **Notice your discomfort.** When you feel defensive or dismissive, pause and get curious about that reaction rather than acting on it.

These practices won't resolve deep conflicts or instantly transform how we process information. But as our Hope continues to demonstrate, even in the midst of one of the world's most intractable conflicts, creating these small bridges of understanding matters. When we make the effort to see beyond our bubbles, we discover not just different information but our shared humanity. And that connection, however fragile, creates the possibility for something new to emerge.

Even when we understand that we all live in different realities, there remains the challenge of maintaining connection across deep value differences. This is perhaps one of the most difficult tests of our ability to assume nothing. To hold space for views that challenge our own without surrendering what matters most to us.

Change is not instantaneous. It starts with small shifts: like a conversation that leaves us questioning our beliefs or a moment of recognition that the other side isn't so different. These shifts build up over time, gradually dismantling the walls of our bubble. Change happens when we allow ourselves to sit with discomfort and listen without judgment.

When we understand the information landscape others inhabit, we can meet them where they are rather than where we imagine them to be.

BREAKING FREE FROM INFORMATION ISOLATION

The purpose of this chapter has been to reinforce the notion that breaking free from our information bubbles doesn't mean abandoning our beliefs. Rather, in doing so, we create space for something powerful to emerge: the joy of connecting through shared experiences that transcend our differences. This brings us to our next step: the transformative power of play.

LET'S PLAY

	State	Step 1	Step 2	Step 3
PRINCIPLE 5 The Rule of Us	From Divided to Connected	Pop the Bubble	Let's Play	It's Okay to Share

I was at a musical show called *Little Rock Story* in Paris recently. The show was created to teach kids the history of rock while reminding their parents how much they love this music too.

There we were, in this very nice theater, seated on our velvety red chairs. Next to us was an elegant French couple with their similarly elegant kids, in nicely ironed trousers and shirts, with clean polished shoes. They were sitting silently in their proper outfits, calmly waiting. They made no eye contact with us, their neighbors; no greeting, no visible excitement or joy of being there.

We were a family of five, with our three kids ages eight, ten, and thirteen, all impatiently waiting, looking around, trying to make eye contact with our neighbors or start a conversation, and struggling to contain our excitement over the concert about to start. We were ready to jump out of our chairs and dance to the music, and very much wanted to share this excitement with the people around us. But we were unsuccessful, since the French family ignored our efforts and kept inside their own world.

It almost seemed like there was an invisible wall between us. The French family was polite but distant, maintaining a reserved demeanor. But as the notes of "Me and the Devil Blues" by Robert Johnson began to fill the theater, a certain sense of a shared experience began to emerge, slowly but surely changing the atmosphere in the theater and between us and our neighbors.

As the concert continued and the first few notes of "Ticket to Ride" by The Beatles rang through the air, I noticed that our neighbors' shoulders relaxed, their heads started moving, and their hands began clapping to the rhythm of that universally loved song.

The music was beginning to work its magic.

Then came "Satisfaction" by The Rolling Stones.

"Stairway to Heaven" by Led Zeppelin.

"Purple Rain" by Prince.

The family made more eye contact with us, their kids started dancing with ours, and soon happy smiles were exchanged between the adults.

It struck me how universal these songs were. Each one seemed to unlock a different memory or feeling, not just for me but for them too. I could see tears of nostalgia and the joy of happy memories on their faces, and it became clear that these melodies, which had accompanied the important moments of so many of our lives, were creating a bridge between us.

By the end of the show, when David Bowie's "Life on Mars?" began, we were all dancing together, holding hands, and there were tears of happiness in all our eyes. Suddenly I felt someone's arms around me. It was the reserved French woman seated next to me, hugging me with all her might, which is a huge sign of trust and affection in France. If I hadn't already had tears in my eyes, this sign of affection and connection would have certainly taken me over the edge.

At that moment, the music had done what words possibly could not. It stripped away all the layers of formality and reserve, revealing our shared love for these songs and the memories they brought. The lyrics, the melodies, and the sense of shared nostalgia had allowed us to connect in a way that was genuine and deeply human.

Music connected us.

That rock concert taught me something I hadn't expected: Sometimes we need to stop talking and just be together. Music gave us a bridge when words couldn't. We didn't need to explain or justify or convince. We just moved to the same rhythm.

Music is just one way to get there. It happens through art, through play, through working side by side toward something we all want. In those moments, the barriers between us feel solid when we're debating, but they turn out to be paper-thin.

It doesn't take profound words or grand gestures. Sometimes it's a song. Sometimes it's a laugh. Sometimes it's mah-jongg tiles clicking on a table in Chengdu. When have you connected with someone not through talking but through doing something together?

TIME TO PLAY

Stephen Nachmanovitch, a musician and author, writes about improvisation and creativity in his book *Free Play: Improvisation in Life and Art*. One thing he says has stayed with me: "When we improvise together, we can experience a bond that is both more profound and more playful than the everyday, ordinary bonds of friendship or acquaintance."

When we play together, whether it's music, sports, art, or just goofing around, something shifts. Play bypasses all the talking and analyzing. It speaks directly to our shared humanity. We stop performing our usual roles. We're not the successful executive or the concerned parent or the person with strong political views. We're just people trying to keep a rhythm going or make something work or not fall over laughing.

In play, we let go of our egos and expectations. We become fully present and receptive to each other. This openness is what makes genuine connection possible, even between people who might otherwise struggle to find common ground.

This doesn't mean we ignore our real differences or the difficult issues we need to address. But play creates a foundation of connection that makes addressing those differences possible. When we've laughed together, struggled together, created something together, we see each other differently. The walls come down just enough.

Play is universal. A child in Ukraine, a grandmother in China, a teenager in California: We all respond to rhythm, to movement, to creating something together. These moments create bonds that can hold even when we disagree about everything else.

We all have seen it work: Improv comedy where strangers become collaborators in minutes. Soccer games that mix people who would never otherwise meet. Jam sessions where language barriers disappear. Dance floors where age and background don't matter.

We're too busy trying to hit the ball or match the beat or not mess up the punch line to worry about being right. And in that state, real connection becomes possible.

IT'S OKAY TO SHARE

*	State	Step 1	Step 2	Step 3
PRINCIPLE 5 The Rule of Us	From Divided to Connected	Pop the Bubble	Let's Play	It's Okay to Share

I was present at a political conference in Paris where two representatives, one from a right-leaning and the other from a left-leaning party, shared the stage. These politicians had frequently clashed in the press and in public debates, their anger and hostility toward each other on full display.

However, something remarkable happened during this conference. The moderator began asking personal questions that had nothing to do with politics or policy but that focused on their lives, their struggles, and their humanity. To my surprise, both politicians responded with candor.

One shared stories of his children and his daily life. The other followed suit, talking about his own family. Each ultimately revealed something deeply personal: Both had experienced the devastating loss of a child. In that moment, the atmosphere in the room shifted. The audience sat in hushed silence, witnessing a profound transformation unfold on stage. The two politicians, who were so often adversaries, connected in a way that transcended their political differences.

They acknowledged each other's pain. They saw each other not as rivals but as fellow human beings who had endured unimaginable loss. The divide between them seemed to narrow as they shared this common ground of grief and resilience. After the session, I noticed the two of them standing together in the corner of the room. They were no longer debating or posturing but talking quietly, their body language warm and friendly. They stood close to each other, their conversation private but visibly meaningful.

While I can't say for certain that this exchange will resolve their political differences, I am hopeful. Vulnerability allowed them to build a bridge, and that bridge might just help them engage with each other in a more understanding and compassionate way moving forward.

Vulnerability is transformative. When we allow ourselves to be open, when we share our pain, our struggles, and our truths, we create the conditions for connection. Vulnerability doesn't mean we always agree with the other person. It doesn't erase our differences or conflicts. But it does create space for compassion and understanding. It helps us see the humanity in one another, even when we stand on opposite sides of an issue.

COMPASSION AND VULNERABILITY

We cannot truly see another person without using compassion. And we can't talk about compassion without acknowledging Brené Brown and her profound work on vulnerability. She wisely said that it is our imperfections that connect us to one another and to our humanity. Buddhist teacher Pema Chödrön echoes this sentiment in her book *The Places That Scare You: A Guide to Fearlessness in Difficult Times*. She writes, "Only when we know our own darkness well can we be present with the darkness of others. Compassion becomes real when we recognize our shared humanity."

Both Brown and Chödrön remind us that vulnerability (being able to share our own darkness) is not weakness; rather, it is a bridge to connection and understanding. Vulnerability and empathy are about embracing our imperfections and sharing them with others in an authentic way.

When I share my struggles, doubts, and imperfections instead of only showing my polished self, people respond differently. Not with judgment but with recognition. "I see you, and I understand, because it happened to me too," their eyes seem to say. Even across vast differences in culture, belief, or experience, vulnerability creates an opening.

We must be willing to stay in vulnerability as a practice. By practicing vulnerability ourselves, we can slowly change the culture of our relationships, families, and even our workplaces to allow for more compassion. When we openly discuss our doubts, discomforts, pain, and even grief, we allow connection to take place.

EXPERIENCES IN VULNERABILITY AND CONNECTION

It started on a sunny day in March 2024. I was about to step onto the stage of a grand conference hall in Sofia, Bulgaria, where high ceilings, soft-blue walls, and glowing lights made the space feel vast and impersonal. The audience consisted of impeccably dressed women in sharp suits and tailored dresses, their confidence radiating in their poised appearances and perfect hairstyles. These women, CEOs, high-level executives, and regional business leaders, sat stiffly around round tables, immersed in their phones or avoiding eye contact. No small talk, no laughter, no exchanges of business cards.

The organizers had poured their energy into creating this two-day event to build a supportive network of female leaders, one that fostered collaboration, mentorship, and trust. Yet, by the second day, it was clear the attendees weren't connecting. The vision of the organizers, warmth, openness, and authentic exchanges, felt out of reach.

The organizers, clearly worried, shared their concerns with me before my keynote began. I understood their worry and felt the weight of their expectations. My opening keynote was designed to set the tone for the day, and later, I would lead a workshop. I stood at the edge of the stage, looking out at the audience: similarly accomplished women, perfectly put together, yet strangely distant from one another.

In that moment, I felt a wave of doubt. What could I possibly do to shift the energy in this room? If these brilliant, capable women weren't naturally connecting, how could I create the conditions for them to do so? I stepped onto the stage, ready to deliver my keynote on "Connective Cultures," where I explore the profound possibility of seeing shared humanity in one another, celebrating each other's uniqueness, and cultivating the essential skills needed to work, live, and love people who are different from us. But as I scanned the room, I just kept feeling the distance, both emotional and physical.

And then I understood their discomfort. I knew what it felt like to be in their shoes, at a crowded event, expected to network and connect, when all you want is to retreat into your own space. I often feel that same resistance, preferring the comfort of solitude, a good book, or a quiet walk in nature. So, I decided to vocalize what I was feeling. Instead of delivering my usual presentation, I stepped off the stage and walked among the attendees. I became one of them.

"Let's figure this out together," I said, breaking the ice. "What's keeping us from connecting?"

I decided to lead by sharing my own vulnerability, admitting how intimidating it was to stand before such accomplished women. "But isn't it funny how we can all feel the same discomfort in trying to connect, no matter how successful we are?" A ripple of nods and smiles followed, softening the tension in the room.

Then I did what I do when I dance tango: I improvised. Instead of sticking to my plan, I let the moment guide me, responding to what the group actually needed. Two exercises changed how these women saw each other.

Breaking Down Barriers with Eye Gazing

I began with a simple exercise: eye gazing. I paired the women and asked them to stand across from each other, making uninterrupted eye contact for two minutes. There was hesitation at first, nervous smiles, glances toward the floor, but slowly, faces softened. Barriers came down. A few women teared up; others burst into laughter. This exercise has now become a cornerstone of my workshops. Eye gazing creates vulnerability without words while building a foundation of trust.

From there, I asked everyone to share a personal story about a moment when they felt disconnected or excluded, or a time they may have excluded someone else. These stories poured out. One woman shared how she often felt like an imposter in male-dominated boardrooms; another spoke of the guilt she carried for dismissing a younger colleague's ideas.

When we discussed how many of us in school were either bullies, were bullied, or were bystanders, one woman hesitated before standing up. Her voice shook as she admitted she had been the bully in middle school. She shared that she had never confessed this to anyone before but felt safe and compelled to share it now. As she spoke, her relief was palpable, and the group embraced her vulnerability without judgment, a powerful moment of collective understanding.

This sharing turned the tables. The women, who had been so closed off before, were now leaning in, nodding, and expressing empathy. The air in the room felt warmer, charged with a new energy of understanding and curiosity.

The Tango of Connection

We then moved into an activity I call the Tango of Connection. I explained that we wouldn't be doing the complex dance sequences most people associate with tango, though in reality, authentic tango is fully improvised rather than choreographed, a perfect metaphor for connection.

"This isn't about dancing expertise," I reassured them. "It's about experiencing connection through movement."

As I turned on the music, the soft, passionate notes of the tango "Poema" by Francisco Canaro and Roberto Maida filling the room, I asked the women to form pairs and demonstrated a simplified version with a volunteer. This particular song, with its gentle rhythm but full of emotion, creates the perfect atmosphere for vulnerability and connection.

I showed them how to stand in an open embrace position, palms lightly touching, maintaining eye contact.

"The goal isn't to execute perfect dance moves," I explained, "but to practice the essential skills of connection: clear intention, active listening through touch, and responding to subtle cues."

The pairs stood facing each other, and the room filled with light steps and focused expressions as each partner experienced the roles of leading and following.

At first, pairs were tasked with deciding who would lead and who would follow. Leaders practiced walking with confidence, offering clear direction without hesitation, while followers learned to step backward, something requiring complete trust in their partner. Then the roles reversed, and the pairs experienced how challenging and humbling it could be to relinquish control or to take charge.

But the most profound moment came during the final activity: Shared Flow. Partners moved together without predefined roles, mirroring and responding to each other's movements, with no words spoken. The room buzzed with nervous energy at first, but soon, laughter and lightness emerged. Watching the women move together, each attuned to the subtle cues of their partner, was a powerful metaphor for collaboration.

"We do this every day," I told them. "In conversations, we're constantly leading and following, initiating and responding. The key is to listen both to yourself and to others, and to build something together that's greater than what we could achieve alone."

Transformations in Sofia

By the end of the session, the room was unrecognizable. The once-cold, formal space now felt like a warm campfire. Women were flushed with joy, laughter rang out, and business cards and hugs were exchanged. Some cried; others laughed. Nobody wanted to leave.

One participant came to me afterward and said, "This was the most impactful session I've ever attended. I've never felt this connected to a group of people in such a short time."

One of the organizers sat down next to me, eyes still bright. "I've been organizing these events for eight years, and I've never seen anything like this. These are women who run companies, sit on boards, manage hundreds of people, and they walked in here terrified of being vulnerable with each other. You showed them it was safe. More than safe: necessary. I think you changed how we'll run every event going forward."

UNIVERSAL LESSONS IN COLLABORATION

This experience at the workshop in Sofia was not unique. In Munich, I watched a room full of conservative German entrepreneurs struggle with the idea of staring into strangers' eyes. "This feels too intimate," one managing director whispered to his wife. "We don't do this kind of thing."

Thirty minutes later, that same man was in tears. He wasn't sad. He'd seen something in the other person's face that he recognized. The exercise had paired him with someone whose political views he'd dismissed entirely during the morning session. "I saw my son in his face," he told me afterward. "My son at five years old, asking me why people were mean to him at school."

In Hong Kong, during a workshop in Mandarin focused on resolving intergenerational family business conflicts, I witnessed the same transformation. Eye gazing bridged decades of tension between fathers and sons, while storytelling fostered mutual respect. In Beijing, in a four-hour experience, bilingual slides ensured inclusivity, allowing participants to engage deeply in conversations about cultural biases.

I now lead workshops and experiences on collaboration, relationships, and intimacy all over the world that last from one-hour short introductions to two full-day retreats, with different focuses: teamwork, conflict resolution, partnerships, or relationships being some of them. Across countries and cultures, I've found that the principles of collaboration remain the same: vulnerability, presence, listening, and improvisation. What changes is the context: the unique fears, biases, and dynamics each group brings into the room.

Leading these workshops showed me that connection isn't a skill reserved for extroverts or those who network effortlessly. It's a practice, a daily choice to show up authentically, to be vulnerable, and to listen without judgment.

In Sofia, I saw powerful women shed their armor and connect as humans. In Hong Kong, I watched generations reconcile. And every time,

I'm reminded why this work matters: because collaboration is not just a professional skill. It's a lifeline to our shared humanity.

This is why I keep traveling, facilitating, and refining. Each session reminds me that despite cultural differences, language barriers, or professional titles, we are all capable of creating something extraordinary when we listen, trust, and step into the flow of collaboration together.

THE EXPANDING CIRCLE

When we truly collaborate despite disagreement, the boundaries between people don't disappear. We remain separate individuals with our own perspectives. But something new emerges from our union, something neither of us could create alone. This mutual collaboration generates possibilities that didn't exist before.

This is the essence of the rule of us. It's not about erasing our differences or pretending conflicts don't exist. It's about expanding our sense of who belongs in our circle of concern, who deserves our empathy, who is part of "us" rather than "them." When we pop our information bubbles, we begin to understand perspectives different from our own. When we play together, we create emotional connections that transcend our intellectual divisions. And when we share ourselves authentically, we discover the common humanity beneath our differences.

I think about that painful moment when Russia invaded Ukraine, and how easy it would have been to retreat into anger and division. The path of "us versus them" felt natural, even justified. But the rule of us showed me something more powerful: the possibility of collaboration even across profound differences and deep pain.

These three elements of the rule of us work together as an integrated practice. Popping our bubbles creates understanding that makes meaningful interaction possible. Play and shared activities build emotional bonds that transcend our differences. And vulnerability creates trust that allows deeper collaboration to flourish. When all three come together, even the most challenging divides can transform into opportunities for collaboration.

What I find so liberating about this practice is that it doesn't ask us to abandon our values or ignore real injustices. It simply invites us to recognize our common humanity even with those we deeply disagree with.

There's freedom in this recognition. A release from the exhausting burden of division and a discovery of possibilities that only emerge when we collaborate despite disagreement.

Reassurance: You Can Keep Your Values

One concern I hear frequently is, "If I become too understanding of other perspectives, will I lose my own convictions? Will I become wishy-washy about things that really matter to me?"

The opposite is actually true. The people I know who are most skilled at loving conflict are also the clearest about their values. When you're not afraid of disagreement, you can be more honest about what you truly believe.

Loving conflict doesn't mean agreeing with everyone to keep the peace or abandoning your principles to avoid tension. What it does mean is being curious about why others hold different values while expressing your own without attacking others for theirs.

I've found that my values have become stronger, not weaker, through loving conflict. When someone challenges my beliefs, I'm forced to examine why I hold them. You don't have to choose between loving conflict and staying true to yourself.

SEE "US" INSTEAD OF "THEM"

Even in our deepest divisions, we can choose to look for what connects us rather than what separates us. When war broke out in Ukraine, I felt this challenge personally. As a Ukrainian watching Russia, whose language is my mother tongue, become the aggressor, I wanted clear lines between allies and enemies. Yet I discovered that when I asked Russian friends about their fears rather than their positions, when we shared music or meals together, when I showed vulnerability despite my anger, collaboration emerged where division had seemed inevitable. Even in our most divided moments, we can train ourselves to see the common humanity that exists alongside our real differences.

Practice bridging division through three approaches that help during conflict:

- First, step outside your information bubble.
- Next, do something together (share a meal, attend an event, work on a project).

- Finally, share something real; be vulnerable.

These actions aren't about abandoning your perspective but seeing the humanity that exists alongside differences.

This week, choose one divisive issue in your life where you feel distance from others with different views. Create a small experiment in collaboration: First, write down what you believe the "other side" thinks and why. Then, find someone who holds that perspective and simply ask, "What matters most to you about this issue?" Listen without planning your response. Notice if anything surprises you about what they share. After your conversation, reflect on what emotions arose in you, both comfortable and uncomfortable ones. Did you discover anything you shared that surprised you? What new possibilities might emerge when you actively look for collaboration across your own divides?

Reassurance: You're Already Doing This

As we reach the end of our time together, I want to remind you of something important: You already know how to love conflict. Every time you've stayed curious instead of getting defensive, every moment you've chosen to understand rather than judge, every conversation where you found common ground across differences. You were practicing these principles.

This book didn't teach you something foreign. It suggested language and structure for the wisdom you already carry. Trust yourself. And remember that loving conflict isn't about perfection. It's about choosing connection over comfort, one conversation at a time.

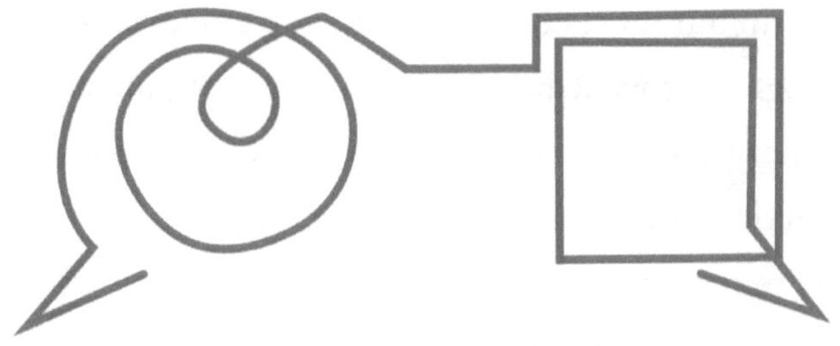

PART III

WHEN CONFLICT BECOMES COLLABORATION

Throughout this book, we've been learning to love conflict as the pathway to genuine collaboration. We've walked through five principles that help us transform our most challenging disagreements into opportunities for breakthrough. But what happens when we integrate all these principles? What emerges when presence, curiosity, deep listening, thoughtful questioning, and the rule of us come together?

Something remarkable occurs. We begin to truly see each other. Not in spite of our conflicts, but because of them.

Every disagreement becomes a doorway. Every heated moment becomes an opportunity to discover something we couldn't have learned any other way.

This is what happens when we stop avoiding conflict and start loving it.

In these final chapters, I want to share what's become clear to me through years of practice: how to see our shared humanity, what tango has taught me about collaboration, and how this might show up in your own life and relationships. This is where the principles come together, in moments that can transform not just how we connect with others but how we understand ourselves.

Chapter 3

FINDING OUR SHARED HUMANITY

Here's what I've learned: the quality of our lives is largely determined by the quality of our relationships. And the quality of those relationships? That's intimacy. Not romance, but the courage to stay connected through difference. To see others as they truly are and allow them to see us. To hold tension without letting it break the bond between us.

If you've made it through all five principles and you're starting to see conflict as opportunity rather than threat, thank you for practicing alongside me. You might be ready for what I think of as the advanced practice.

This isn't about handling disagreements that come your way anymore. This is about actively creating necessary conflict. Speaking up in meetings when you see problems others are avoiding. Having the conversation with your teenager that you've been putting off. Addressing the team dynamic everyone can feel but no one wants to name.

This is where it gets hard. It's one thing to respond skillfully when someone else starts a difficult conversation. It's another thing entirely to be the one who initiates it.

The conflicts you avoid creating are often the ones that could transform your relationships, your work, your family dynamics. The conversation you're not having is probably the one everyone is waiting for someone to be brave enough to start.

You've built the skills. You know how to engage with presence, question your assumptions, listen to understand, ask from curiosity, and see shared humanity. Now the question is: Are you willing to use them proactively instead of just reactively?

SEE THE CHILD

Remember the eye-gazing exercise I tried in Sofia that has now become one of the cornerstones of my experiences and workshops? There's one instruction that transforms it from a simple connection practice into something much more powerful.

After a workshop in Berlin, I switched things up. Instead of pairing people randomly, I asked them to find someone whose views really challenged them. A startup founder with someone who thought entrepreneurs were greedy. A religious person with an atheist. A climate activist with a climate skeptic. Then we did the same eye gazing.

But of all the suggestions I've tried, the strongest moments come from one instruction in particular: "Look for the little kid inside the other person. Imagine them being five years old. How did they look? What were they up to? What was their life like? What happened to them? What did they lose? Did they have love? How did it affect them?"

This is the secret of loving conflict. When you see the child in someone, you can disagree with their position while staying curious about their story. You can hold your ground while holding their humanity. The conflict doesn't disappear, but it transforms into something generative.

What might change in your relationships if you practiced looking for the child in everyone you meet, including yourself?

The practice of seeing the child becomes a natural extension of the five principles we've explored throughout this book. It helps us engage with true presence, assume nothing about another's experience, listen to understand rather than respond, question with genuine interest, and recognize our fundamental connection as human beings. It reminds us that collaboration isn't just something we do. It's a way of seeing that transforms every interaction. When we try to see the little child in others, our hearts start to warm, our defenses disappear, and we become more receptive to their presence. We are better able to think clearly, and we start to sense their emotions and intentions beyond surface appearances. We begin to wonder what they might be afraid of. We are then able to be kind toward them, feel and show respect, and pose curious questions when we do begin to speak.

The eye-gazing exercises never fail to astound me with the level of connection achieved without anyone saying a word. After the exercises, I bring everyone together as a group to share experiences. Participants often express feelings of closeness and understanding toward their partners, even if they'd never met before. Many share that they felt loved and loving, seen and seeing, listened to and listening.

And this leads to collaboration. So try it out. On others or on yourself.

Now It's Your Turn

The eye-gazing exercise shows us what's possible when we truly see another person. But you don't need a workshop to practice this. You can start seeing the child in people during your everyday conflicts, and it changes everything.

I used to think this was just a nice exercise for retreats. Then I started using it during the actual disagreements in my daily life. When my business partner challenged my entire strategy in front of our team, instead of getting defensive, I paused and looked at his face. I imagined him as a seven-year-old, probably the kid who always had his hand up in class, eager to share his ideas. Suddenly, his criticism didn't feel like an attack. It felt like enthusiasm.

This practice isn't just about connection. It's about loving conflict enough to stay curious when things get heated. Here's how to start:

- **Start with someone easy.** Pick a person you disagree with but don't actively dislike. Maybe a coworker with different approaches or a family member with different values. During your next conversation, silently ask yourself: "What was this person like as a child? What did they love? What scared them? What experiences shaped who they became?"

- **Notice what shifts in your body.** When you see the child in someone, everything changes. Your shoulders might relax. Your voice might get softer. Your curiosity might get stronger. You might stop trying to win and start trying to understand.

- **Try it during actual conflict.** This is where it gets interesting. The next time someone challenges your ideas or questions your decisions, pause before responding. Look at their face and imagine them as a child in school, hoping they have the right answer. This doesn't mean agreeing with them. It means seeing their humanity while you hold your ground.

- **Practice with people who really trigger you.** Choose someone whose beliefs make your blood pressure rise. Someone whose politics or lifestyle choices you find incomprehensible. Spend a few minutes imagining their childhood. What pain or joy might have shaped such different values? You're not excusing their views. You're expanding your capacity to engage with them.

- **Don't forget yourself.** When you catch yourself getting defensive during conflict, connect with your own child. What is that five-year-old afraid of? What does that child need to feel safe enough to stay curious instead of reactive?

This practice transforms conflict from something we endure into something we can actually learn from. The disagreement doesn't disappear, but it becomes a doorway instead of a wall.

See the Child in Yourself

There are times when we have a problem connecting with ourselves. Especially in moments when we are dissatisfied with how we behaved in a certain situation. Then we can become very critical of ourselves, right? When that happens to me, I use this "see the child" exercise as a trick on myself, especially at times when I am feeling stuck, am on the defense, or in disagreement or conflict with someone.

When that happens to me, I imagine myself as a kid, a five-year old child. I even have a name for myself based on how my parents, brother, and grandma addressed me when I was little: Annushka, Anechka, Annyuta. Calling myself one of these names immediately brings me back to kindness and self-love. Which is so very necessary, since *I believe that our inner voice, how we talk to and treat ourselves, is reflected in how we talk to and treat others.*

Our inner dialogue shapes our interactions with the world. Cultivating kindness toward ourselves allows us to extend genuine compassion to others, fostering deeper collaborations and understanding.

EXTREME LISTENING

In the vast landscape of listening, *extreme listening* stands as the pinnacle, a jewel in the crown of communication. It's the top skill, the ultimate practice that takes listening to its highest level. Documentary filmmaker Deeyah Khan does something remarkable. She practices extreme listening with people whose beliefs directly threaten her existence. Her work with white supremacists and extremists proves the transformative potential of listening at its most courageous level. Her life exemplifies that extreme listening goes beyond hearing words; it seeks to uncover the human stories and emotions behind even the most polarizing ideologies.

Deeyah Khan's presence is striking. She is always poised and confident, and has expressive eyes that reflect both empathy and determination. Whether on screen or at events, she embodies the very essence of the empathy and respect she stands for.

An Emmy- and Peabody Award–winning filmmaker and human rights activist, Khan was born in Norway to immigrant parents from Afghanistan and Pakistan. Growing up facing discrimination and threats shaped everything about her work.

To Khan, extreme listening means trying to understand people's humanity rather than confront their beliefs head on. It involves creating a safe space for dialogue, listening without judgment, and seeking to understand the "why" behind someone's beliefs.

Key principles of extreme listening include:

- **Create a safe environment.** Ensure that the other person feels respected and heard.

- **Practice active and nonjudgmental listening.** Fully focus on the speaker without forming rebuttals or judgments.

- **Seek the "why."** Explore the underlying reasons for someone's beliefs and behaviors.

- **Find common ground.** Identify shared values or experiences to build mutual respect and empathy.

What Khan practices is the ultimate form of loving conflict. She doesn't avoid these dangerous conversations. She seeks them out. She doesn't try to change these men's minds. She tries to understand their hearts. And somehow, through that willingness to engage rather than dismiss, real transformation happens.

One of Khan's most moving documentaries is *White Right: Meeting the Enemy*, where she sits down with white supremacists and fascists to uncover the personal stories and vulnerabilities behind their hatred. Rather than dismissing these men as monsters, she's determined to discover the people behind the masks. While she reveals the human beings behind the extremist facades, Khan most probably also finds her own prejudices challenged and her own tolerance tested.

As I watched the movie, I wondered: Can Khan find it within her to try and befriend the fascists she meets? Will her empathy extend to neo-Nazis? Even when they declare, to her face, that she is, effectively, sub-human? And, most importantly, could I do the same if I was in her place? In her work, Khan emphasizes the importance of creating a space where individuals feel heard and respected, even when their views are controversial or offensive.

Without a doubt, engaging with individuals who hold extremist views can be extremely challenging. That's why I watch and rewatch her films: to remind me of her commitment to extreme listening. It not only offers us a powerful tool for bridging divides but also provides hope of creating a space for respectful and nonjudgmental dialogue; hope that if both parties would use these tools, there might be a possibility of understanding the humanity behind the ideology and finding common ground.

Khan often highlights the importance of listening without judgment, allowing individuals to share their stories and perspectives fully. Here is some advice from Khan:

- "You don't have to agree with them. You don't even have to like them. But if you show up with a willingness to listen, you might find common ground."
- "It's not about changing their mind on the spot but about respecting their dignity and humanity in the conversation."
- "When you meet someone face-to-face, it's harder to hate them. You start to see the person behind the ideology."
- "Sharing personal experiences, rather than statistics or arguments, helps break down barriers and fosters empathy."

Khan's work reminds us that at the heart of listening lies the power to bridge divides and transform relationships. Through her films, she offers a roadmap for bridging divides and creating spaces for dialogue rooted in dignity and respect.

Thank you, Deeyah Khan, for your inspiration. I am sure I will be rewatching one of your films again soon. And practicing "extreme listening" over and over again.

Practicing Extreme Listening on My Own

Inspired by Deeyah Khan's work, I've found myself reflecting on how her principles of extreme listening can be applied to my own experiences. One moment, in particular, stands out: a time when I was confronted with beliefs that clashed so deeply with my own that I struggled to see the person behind the ideology.

I was attending an interfaith gathering at a historic religious site, a place known for its beauty and rich traditions. I brought my children to expose them to diverse perspectives and the architectural grandeur of the space. As we listened to one of the speakers, a religious leader declared from the stage that women hold only half the value of men. I was furious. My children were there, and that made me even angrier. I wanted to shield them from these ideas and take them somewhere safe.

Yet, we stayed. The more he talked, the angrier I got. My pulse quickened, my body felt tight, and my thoughts became a whirlpool of rage: How dare he say this in front of my children? How can anyone listen to this? I stopped seeing him as a human being and started viewing him as the embodiment of ideas I was passionately against. He became "the enemy."

These feelings separated me from everyone around me. From my children, from the people in the audience. I was overwhelmed and flooded by them. I was not fully present there anymore. And as such, I could not really think or act. Then I remembered the faces of people in Deeyah Khan's documentaries: faces filled with hatred yet softened under her empathetic gaze. I thought of her composed, kind presence and decided to apply her principles, starting with myself.

I took a deep breath and asked myself: What is my "why" here? What do I care about right now? I looked around and saw the faces of other people in the audience. I noticed puzzlement, incomprehension, confusion, anger, aloofness, sadness, surprise, agreement, understanding, each face telling its own story. That thought helped me connect with the people in the room. I also saw the faces of my children, who were gazing at the ornate ceiling, marveling at the intricate carvings. They weren't even listening; they were simply enjoying the beauty of the space.

That reminded me what was most important for me at that moment: my children. Their experience mattered more to me than anything else. I then focused my attention back on the speaker on stage. What is his story and his "why"? I knew nothing about him. What would it take for me to have a conversation with him? Would he talk to me, openly and sincerely? Could I tell him how his words made me feel? How all my life I strived to contribute to building a better, more equal society for us and our children, and how hearing his words about women's lesser value upset and infuriated but also deeply scared me?

I couldn't hold a dialogue with the person on stage right there and then. What I could do is be there with my children, and try and see the common humanity in people around me. And then decide if there is a way to go into a dialogue with this religious leader at some more appropriate time, if it is what I wanted to do. But there, at that moment, my focus was to stay present with the people I was with. And to be deliberate about what I did next. Later, I chose to learn more about him, his upbringing, his culture, the origins of his beliefs and possible biases, so that if and when we do speak, I can come into the dialogue more informed, and more open to real collaboration. That process is still unfolding. The story isn't finished yet.

SEEING HUMANITY BEHIND IDEOLOGY

What the eye-gazing exercise and Deeyah Khan's practice of extreme listening have in common is that they remind us that we will not love conflict until we learn to use it as a tool for understanding. They are not about debating or agreeing. They are tools to use to create a space where collaboration and understanding can thrive, even in the face of profound differences.

Conflict challenges us to see the humanity in the other person, no matter how different their beliefs may be from our own. My experiences with eye gazing in my workshops and Khan's work inspire me to approach even the most difficult conversations with curiosity and composure. I try to remind myself to see the child in the other person and to listen to understand.

Chapter 4

DEVELOPING THE SKILLS OF LOVING CONFLICT

I used to think that quality of performance came only from talent. Now I know it comes from putting in the hours. Quantity of practice can lead to mastery. I didn't always understand this, at least not consciously.

You may have heard the axiom that it takes ten thousand hours of practice to excel at anything, whether that be a sport, craft, or anything that involves skill. While the exact number is debatable, we can agree that it takes a long time to become skillful at anything, whether or not we have an inherent talent in that area. Practice, practice, practice is how I've mastered five languages and become an accomplished entrepreneur.

Quantity can become quality, especially when you have the power of inspiration to keep you going. But the going isn't always easy. Here are some ways to make that learning journey easier.

SIGNS THAT YOU'RE LEARNING TO LOVE CONFLICT

When I started this journey, I was terrified of disagreement. Now, many years later, I can feel the difference in my body when conflict arises. Here's what I noticed about myself as I got more comfortable with conflict; I hope some of this will be true for you as well:

- Conflict energizes me instead of draining me. Before, a tense conversation would leave me exhausted. Now, when I stay present and curious, I often feel more alive afterward.

- I catch myself getting excited about different perspectives. Last week, someone challenged my entire approach to business. Instead of getting defensive, I found myself thinking, "Oh, this is interesting. What can I learn here?"

- I stop taking disagreement personally. When someone pushes back on my ideas, I don't hear "You're wrong" anymore. I hear "Here's another way to look at this."

- I find myself creating conflict where I used to avoid it. I ask the question everyone's thinking but nobody wants to voice. I bring up the issue the team keeps dancing around. I choose to engage. That's what loving conflict looks like in practice.

- I notice my relationships getting deeper, not easier. The people closest to me might say I've become more challenging to be around, but also more real.

- I start seeing conflict as information, not attack. When my teenager slams the door, I wonder what they're trying to tell me instead of just feeling hurt.

These aren't signs that I (or you!) have "mastered" conflict. They're signs of falling in love with it. And that changes everything about how you move through the world.

After my family moved to Paris, I continued to pursue my love of tango. And one chilly October afternoon I had a profound experience that taught me an important lesson about conflict and collaboration. I was at a friendly milonga (a social tango gathering) when a man I didn't know approached me and held out his hand. Usually I prefer to watch potential partners dance before agreeing to a *tanda* (a set of three or four dances), but his gentle gesture made it hard to decline. By the end of the first dance, I realized my mistake. His hand pressed too hard on my lower back, and it hurt. The abruptness of his lead felt like someone yelling at me. I couldn't relax and enjoy the dance.

I gathered up my courage and asked him to loosen his pressure on my back. His reply: "This is how true connection in tango feels," he said curtly. "If you don't like it, I guess we'll have to stop dancing together." I simply nodded and stepped away before the *tanda* was finished, something that is rarely done in tango.

A few moments later, I was seated next to an elegant older woman. "I feel so terrible," I confessed. "He said I don't understand the true connection of tango. Maybe I shouldn't have said anything."

She looked at me seriously. "If something makes you uncomfortable or crosses your boundaries, you have every right to speak up," she said. "Connection should never come at the cost of your comfort or well-being."

Her words hit me like a revelation. Too often in my life, I had prioritized staying connected over protecting my own needs. Now, a key message I always strive to convey is that true connection is built on mutual respect, not sacrifice.

USING REFLECTION TO GROW YOUR SKILLS

We do not see things as they are.
We see things as we are.

—ANAÏS NIN

We all bring our history into every conflict. Our backgrounds, cultures, beliefs, and biases shape not just what we argue about but how we argue.

This is why I reflect regularly on who I am, how I've grown, and what I've learned. Reflection helps me identify patterns, recognize growth, and see my biases more clearly. It's not about finding perfect answers. It's about having the courage to ask myself meaningful questions.

Here are three methods that work for me.

#1 Return to Places That Stay the Same

When I lived in Mill Valley, I hiked to Cascade Falls almost every day for twelve years. I knew every tree, hill, and bridge on that trail. Now that I live in Paris, I try to get back at least once a year.

Nelson Mandela said, "There is nothing like returning to a place that remains unchanged to find the ways in which you yourself have altered." He's right. The familiarity of the place helps me see how much I've changed.

This "place" can be your hometown, a reunion with high school classmates, an old friend who knew you when you were younger, a book you loved in childhood, or a favorite album from an earlier time. They all help you measure yourself against the past.

Is there a place you go that stays the same and makes you see how you've changed?

#2 Establish an Annual Ritual of Self-Reflection

My husband and I have a ritual we maintain every Yom Kippur, the Jewish day of reflection and forgiveness. We go for a long walk, each bringing a notebook. We take turns answering questions, listening without interruption, and taking notes.

- How was your year? What were your most joyful moments? Your moments of fear, sorrow, and disappointment? What did you learn this year?

- Did this year's events change you, and if so, how?

- Have I been supportive of you, and if so, how?

- What do you want to forgive yourself for? What do you want to forgive others for?

- What are your biggest hopes and fears for the next year?

- How can I support you better next year?

This walk is never easy. It's hard to stay precise and present while being vulnerable. It's hard to stay honest while afraid of misunderstandings or rejection. It's hard to listen to the other person's vulnerability without becoming defensive or judgmental.

But the amount of self-reflection we do during these walks is enormous. It leads to growth on a personal level and as a couple.

#3 Write Your Memoir

Writing a memoir is the most obvious path to self-reflection. It allows you to consciously narrate your life, pull up memories of facts and how you interpreted them then, and think about how events and people affected you.

Writing a memoir takes courage. You have to be honest and vulnerable enough to show yourself to others despite the fear of being judged or rejected. But sharing your stories so readers can truly know you, and see their own reflection in your words, can inspire others to do the same.

Here's what I've learned about using reflection to love conflict better. The goal isn't to eliminate your biases. It's to become curious about them. When you catch yourself getting triggered by someone's politics or lifestyle choices, ask yourself: What story am I telling myself about this person? What am I afraid they represent? That's where real learning begins.

DON'T FORGET THE JOY

Joshua Waitzkin's book *The Art of Learning* struck me with its emphasis on falling in love with the process itself, not just fixating on outcomes. As both a chess champion and martial arts world champion, he knows something about mastery. He talks about breaking down complex skills into digestible pieces and practicing them until they become second nature.

What sometimes gets overlooked in conversations about mastery and practice is joy. In all my years of dancing, learning languages, and building businesses, I've found that passion fuels persistence. The hours I've invested in tango weren't just about mechanical repetition. They were filled with delight, curiosity, and love for the dance itself.

This applies to how we connect with others too. The art of truly seeing and hearing another person isn't something we're born knowing how to do perfectly. Don't expect to be an expert at loving conflict the first time you try any of the techniques in this book. It requires practice, lots of practice. Each conversation, each misunderstanding, each moment of genuine collaboration becomes part of learning to be truly present with others.

My journeys through dance floors in Buenos Aires, boardrooms in Shanghai, and family dinners in Paris have shown me that connection, like anything worth doing, gets better with practice. The awkwardness softens. The effort becomes natural.

Eventually, you stop thinking about the steps and just dance.

TANGO AS A MIRROR: LESSONS IN CONFLICT, COLLABORATION, AND FREEDOM

At the start of this book, I was a four-year-old child in a Soviet Ukrainian school room. As I write today, I am a fifty-year-old woman who lives in France and works in China, the United States, and Europe. I am on my third immigration, learning about French culture and society every day, and making many mistakes along the way. I practice the steps that allowed me to develop a love of conflict: I engage with presence, assume nothing, listen to understand, practice the art of questioning, and follow the rule of us. It's a lot of work that takes significant energy and attention. Along the way, there are wins, losses, and challenges.

As you've seen throughout this book, throughout my adulthood, tango has become my laboratory for practicing the principles of collaboration we've explored throughout this book. The dance floor is a microcosm where presence, assumptions, listening, questioning, and shared humanity all come into play with each step and embrace. What looks like a structured dance often reveals itself as a mirror, reflecting back to me the lessons about collaboration I'm still learning in my daily life. One of the most important learning opportunities I discovered through tango began in 2019.

In February 2019, I found myself in Buenos Aires, the capital of tango, on a birthday trip I had gifted myself. I was at Salon Canning, a cult tango venue, attending a traditional milonga where men initiated the dance and women accepted their invitations. Men led. Women followed. That was the rule.

I sat uncomfortably in the area designated for women, playing the role I was assigned to gain the opportunity to dance. I looked wistfully at the lucky dancers on the wooden floor. "Why were they invited and not I?" I wondered, feeling a familiar pang of self-doubt. "What did I do wrong? Am I wearing the right outfit? Am I attractive enough? Is my posture straight enough? Should I smile more?"

The room was rich with red: the décor, the dancers' clothing, the shoes moving elegantly across the floor. "Should I have worn something red?" I thought. "Will anyone please just invite me? I've worked so hard at this dance. I'm good at it! Why can't they see that?"

Another *tanda* passed. (A *tanda* is a set of four songs played consecutively, during which the same pair dances together.) I remained seated on my uncomfortable chair, waiting and smiling at the sea of men who scanned the rows of women as though selecting items from a menu. As I sat there, I found myself questioning everything I'd been taught about tango.

"Why do I need to sit here and wait for a man to choose me? Why can't I initiate? Why is it their privilege to decide who gets to dance?"

The facts of this tradition were weighing heavily on me: The tango has required women to always follow, always surrender, and always wait; men always initiate and lead. Everyone is confined to their roles, developing only the skills assigned to them while never exploring the other side.

And beyond my personal frustration, I thought about the broader implications: Men never got to experience the freedom of following, to relax into the dance and express themselves, and women never had the opportunity to lead, to take responsibility for guiding another person, interpreting the music, and navigating the crowded dance floor. It didn't feel right. It didn't feel fair.

I couldn't sit there and simply accept this tradition. This moment would be my turning point, the moment I decided to question the rules, challenge the status quo, and take action. What would happen if I, a woman, started to lead? What if men were given the chance to follow? What would we learn from breaking these traditional roles?

Sitting in that chair, waiting to be chosen, I faced a choice about conflict. I could accept the tradition quietly, or I could challenge it.

These rebellious questions swirled in my mind as I stood up from that chair, ready to begin a journey I didn't fully understand yet, a journey into the world of leading in tango.

The path forward wasn't easy. I quickly realized that challenging long-held traditions meant facing resistance at every turn.

Yet that night, I chose conflict.

I'd spent months learning how to lead, something that felt unnatural at first. Then I stood up and asked a person to dance. Some people stared. A few were clearly uncomfortable. But I kept going. And I found teachers and a community of people, in Buenos Aires, Paris, and many other cities, who danced both roles, independent of their gender, rule questioners like me. Some even changed roles within a single dance.

Since that night, I have repeated my break with tango tradition. Some milongas asked me to leave the floor when I attempted to lead. Women, accustomed to their role as followers, refused to dance with me not out of malice, but often out of fear. They worried that being seen dancing with a female leader might damage their chances of being invited by men later in the evening.

And then there was my own inner critic, loud and relentless: "Who are you to lead? Do you even have the skills for this?" "What if this confuses or slows your progress as a follower?" "How dare you question a tradition that so many respect and cherish?"

But I kept going. Step by step, I pushed through the discomfort. I practiced endlessly, facing rejection and self-doubt head-on.

And slowly, I began to see the rewards of this rebellion.

LEADING AND FOLLOWING THROUGH CONFLICT

I bring this same lesson about leading and following into my workshops and private sessions, though not everyone is ready for actual tango. In Düsseldorf, I worked with a leadership team where everyone wanted to be in charge and no one wanted to follow.

I introduced them to the concept without any dancing. "In your most successful collaborations," I asked, "when were you leading? When were you following? When were you doing both?"

The breakthrough came when their CEO realized she had been trying to lead everything because she didn't trust anyone to lead her. "I've never learned how to follow skillfully," she admitted. "I either take over completely or I check out completely."

That afternoon, I taught them to practice leading and following through simple exercises. Walking together where one person sets the pace and direction while the other matches their energy. Then switching roles.

We could all see it working. Over the following weeks, their team leader mentioned that meetings were going differently. People seemed to notice when they needed to step up versus when they needed to step back. There was less fighting about who was in charge.

This is what the tango of conflict looks like in practice. Not agreement, but conscious collaboration. Not avoiding disagreement, but dancing with it skillfully.

THE REWARDS OF CREATING CONFLICT

My rebellion wasn't just about tango. It was about every time I'd stayed quiet when I wanted to speak up. Every time I'd accepted "how things are" instead of asking "how they could be."

Learning to lead in tango revealed four things about loving conflict:

- **I learned to walk with purpose while someone walked backward.** When you create conflict by challenging norms, people are walking into unknown territory. You better be clear about where you're going.

- **I became kinder to other people creating change.** Once I knew how hard it is to challenge tradition, I stopped judging others who were trying to do the same thing in their fields.

- **I learned what it means to be responsible for someone else's experience during conflict.** When you initiate difficult conversations, you're asking people to trust you with their vulnerability.

- **I discovered that the most meaningful connections happen when people can question and switch roles.** The best connections are the ones where everyone gets to lead sometimes and follow sometimes.

This is what loving conflict creates. Not agreement. Not harmony. But the freedom to express who you really are while staying curious about who others really are.

What I also realized from my experiences of leading in tango is that I also facilitate the freedom of full expression for my partner. By taking the role of a leader I free up space for someone to step in and follow. I've watched many men over the years of me leading in tango decide they will try following, and being extremely happy and satisfied with their experience and learnings.

In those moments of complete freedom to choose our role and expression, we create something together. We dance what feels right, expressing ourselves and connecting with each other to the beautiful music. We show who we authentically are while intently listening to the other.

By expressing ourselves fully and witnessing the other person do the same, we create something bigger than either of us: art.

This is the fullest expression of loving conflict. When you can lead and follow, when you can initiate and respond, when you can hold your position while staying curious about theirs, you're not just dancing. You're practicing real collaboration. You're loving conflict.

In the end, to be this free, we must pass through every step of The Five Principles of Loving Conflict:

- Engage with presence, seeing what's real, establishing trust carefully and deliberately before we start dancing.

- Assume nothing about our partner, staying curious literally every step of the dance.

- Listen intently. Since this type of dance is an improvisation, my every step is as much an initiation as a continuation of what my partner initiated. I lead and follow at the same time, and so do they.

- Practice the art of questioning. This means being deliberate and interested in our partner, the music, the floor, the other couples.

- Practice the rule of us by creating art together and seeing our common humanity in our every move.

For me, dancing tango in both roles is my metaphor for freedom in life, in relationships, in business. It's breaking free from traditional expectations, being deliberate, intent, present at each moment, and allowing and inspiring others to do the same.

As a tango leader, I practice clear communication, sensitivity to my partner's movements, active listening, and decisive yet collaborative decision-making. These skills transfer directly to relationships and professional environments. They underscore the importance of empathy, mutual respect, and effective communication for building harmonious relationships, whether on the dance floor, at home, or in the boardroom.

These skills remind us that loving conflict isn't about winning or losing. It's about creating something together that neither of us could create alone. So here's my invitation to you: Love deeply. Fight kindly. Stay close. Because that's what this whole journey has been about—learning to stay connected through the moments that usually pull us apart.

FURTHER READING

Part I: The Tango of Conflict and Collaboration

- Haidt, Jonathan. *The Righteous Mind: Why Good People Are Divided by Politics and Religion.* Pantheon Books, 2012. This work is also relevant to the "mastering emotions" topic of Step 1.2.

- Jayawickreme, Eranda. "The Power of Intellectual Humility." In *Radical Humility: Essays on Ordinary Acts,* edited by Rebekah Modrak and Jamie Vander Broek. Belt Publishing, 2021.

Part II: The Five Principles of Loving Conflict

- Alexander Technique for Listening, The. https://alexandertechnique.com.

- Ambady, Nilina, and Robert Rosenthal. "Thin Slices of Expressive Behavior as Predictors of Interpersonal Consequences: A Meta-Analysis." *Psychological Bulletin* 111, no. 2 (1992): 256–74.

- Amiel, Henri-Frédéric. *Amiel's Journal: The Journal Intime of Henri-Frédéric Amiel.* Translated by Mrs. Humphry. Macmillan, 1891. Henri-Frédéric Amiel, a Swiss philosopher and poet, said, "Uncertainty is the refuge of hope." In his *Journal Intime,* Amiel suggested that uncertainty allows hope to flourish. If everything were certain, there would be no room for dreams and aspirations.

- Bernays, Edward. *Propaganda.* Ig Publishing, 1928. I think that Edward Bernays, known as the father of public relations, has some good insights into understanding each other and breaking out of our bubbles.

- Brislin, Richard. *Working with Cultural Differences: Dealing Effectively with Diversity in the Workplace.* Praeger Publishers, 2008.

- Cleveland Clinic. "Parasympathetic Nervous System (PSNS)." Updated June 2022. https://my.clevelandclinic.org/health/body/23266-parasympathetic-nervous-system-psns. Neurological studies suggest that a softer tone can help activate the parasympathetic nervous system, which promotes relaxation and reduces stress. This biological response can help both parties in a conflict feel more at ease and open to finding a resolution.

- Crocker, Jennifer, Kristin Voelkl, Maria Testa, and Brenda Major. "Social Stigma: The Affective Consequences of Attributional Ambiguity." *Emotion* 7, no. 1 (2007): 178–82.

- Daryl Davis. https://www.daryldavis.com.

- Decety, Jean, and Philip L. Jackson. "The Functional Architecture of Human Empathy." *Behavioral and Cognitive Neuroscience Reviews* 3, no. 2 (2004): 71–100.

- Harari, Yuval Noah. *21 Lessons for the 21st Century.* Spiegel & Grau, 2018. In this book, Harari emphasizes the importance of questioning deeply ingrained beliefs.

- Harari, Yuval Noah. *Sapiens: A Brief History of Humankind.* HarperCollins, 2015. This book explains how much of human communication revolves around imagined realities, like nations, corporations, and religions.

- Katie, Byron, and Stephen Mitchell. *Loving What Is: Four Questions That Can Change Your Life.* Harmony, 2002.

- Kosfeld, Michael, Markus Heinrichs, Paul J. Zak, Urs Fischbacher, and Ernst Fehr. "Oxytocin Increases Trust in Humans." *Nature* 435 (2005): 673–76. https://doi.org/10.1038/nature03701. The authors also suggest that the shared neural activity of walking not only enhances empathy but also lays the groundwork for trust and rapport. In fact, the mirror neurons in our brain make sure that even in silence, we are profoundly connected.

- Li, Qing. *Forest Bathing: How Trees Can Help You Find Health and Happiness.* Viking, 2018. This book by Dr. Qing Li, a leading researcher on forest medicine, discusses the therapeutic effects of forests on human health and provides insights into the practice of forest bathing.

- Matsumoto, David, and Hyi-Sung Hwang. "Nonverbal Communication: The Messages of Emotion, Action, Space, and Silence." In *The Routledge Handbook of Language and Intercultural Communication,* edited by Jane Jackson. Routledge, 2012.

- Nickerson, Raymond S. "Confirmation Bias: A Ubiquitous Phenomenon In Many Guises." *Review of General Psychology* 2, no. 2 (1998): 175–220.

- Sunstein, Cass R. *Echo Chambers: Bush v. Gore, Impeachment, and Beyond.* Princeton University Press, 2001.

- Tajfel, Henri, and John C. Turner. "The Social Identity Theory of Intergroup Behavior." In *Psychology of Intergroup Relations,* edited by William G. Austin and Stephen Worchel. Nelson-Hall, 1986.

Part III: When Conflict Becomes Collaboration

- Brown, Brené. *Daring Greatly: How the Courage to Be Vulnerable Transforms the Way We Live, Love, Parent, and Lead.* Gotham, 2012.

- Khan, Deeyah. "Befriending the 'Other': Seeing Beyond Extremism." YouTube, 2023.

- Khan, Deeyah, dir. *White Right: Meeting the Enemy.* Fuuse Film, 2017.

- Sinek, Simon, host. *A Bit of Optimism*, podcast. "Extreme Listening with Deeyah Khan." Simon Sinek Inc., August 10, 2020.

ABOUT THE AUTHOR

ANNA LECAT is an international CEO and entrepreneur, intimacy and conflict consultant, and global speaker. Originally from Ukraine, she has spent twenty-five years leading companies and teams across fashion, manufacturing, and global supply-chain industries. Fluent in Mandarin and four other languages, she built and scaled multinational ventures across China, the United States, and Europe.

Today, she helps leaders, couples, and organizations transform tension into trust through her framework The Five Principles of Loving Conflict, shared on stages worldwide. A passionate tango dancer who leads as often as she follows, Anna lives in France with her husband, three multilingual children, and her parents.